The Addiction Loop

Directing Your Dopamine

THOMAS GODDARD

ISBN: 978-1-971349-15-2

Table of Contents

This book is meant to be used, not just read.

If you're holding *The Addiction Loop*, chances are you've already tried to change your habits, improve your consistency, or "do better"—only to find yourself returning to the same patterns under stress.

This book isn't here to motivate you or fix you.
It's here to help you understand what's actually happening beneath the surface.

Addiction, as it's described here, isn't a moral failure or a lack of discipline. It's a loop—a repeated pattern your nervos system relies on for short-term relief, even when it creates long-term cost. Once you can see that loop clearly, the shame begins to loosen. And when shame loosens, real change becomes possible.

You don't need to read this book in order.
You don't need to finish it.
You don't need to agree with everything inside it.

Let it meet you where you are.
On good days—and especially on low ones.

The Truth Nobody Else Will Tell You About Addiction

My father used to say it is easier to establish a new habit than it is to break an old one, and I spent thirty years proving him wrong before I finally understood he was trying to save my life.

Tonight at hibachi, watching the chef's knives dance like silver birds against the hot metal sky while my daughter's eyes reflect the onion volcano's flame, I finally understand what he meant. The teriyaki steam sweetens the surrounding air, a baby squeals somewhere behind me, strangers cheer as a shrimp arcs through space into an open mouth, and my phone buzzes against the table like it always does, calling me away from this moment into the familiar gravitational pull of escape.

Five seconds pass while the old loop whispers its seductive promise: check the screen, step out of this moment, find your hit of dopamine in whatever digital fix awaits. I feel that familiar tug in my chest, the tiny hook behind my sternum that's been there since I was seventeen, though its bait has changed over the decades from white powder to pixels to endless scrolling. When you're bored and tired and vaguely sad all at once, those feelings blend into a single muddy color that you know exactly how to make disappear, even if only for a minute.

I turn the phone face down and ask my daughter to tell me one small win from her week.

She blinks at the unexpected question, then grins as the chef flips rice into a heart shape that beats once, twice against the grill. She tells me about a teacher who noticed her effort, about finally nailing a tough line in theater, about laughing so hard with friends in the hallway that her stomach hurt for an hour afterward. I mirror her stories back to her and ask another question, feeling the hook in my chest loosen with each word she shares, watching the room warm around us until her face becomes the only screen I need.

Here's what nobody will tell you about addiction: every single one of us is an addict.

Not metaphorically, not poetically, but neurologically and behaviorally. Your brain runs on the same dopamine loops that drove me to snort cocaine in my father's Honda CRX at seventeen, that kept me clicking through pornography while my marriage collapsed around me, that pulls you toward your phone right now even as you're reading these words. The machinery of addiction isn't special or broken in some of us—it's the fundamental operating system of the human brain, as natural as breathing and as powerful as love.

The only question that matters isn't whether you're an addict, but what you're addicted to and whether those addictions are building your life or burning it down.

Split-screen memories flash through my mind as I watch my daughter laugh at the chef's theatrics, each one a moment when I had five seconds to choose between the life I was living and the life I wanted:

A bus bathroom in 1990 where "just a tiny bump" of cocaine before our high school choir competition led to me cracking on my solo, watching my future as a performer dissolve in real time. A stranger in a Chattanooga dive bar who looked straight through my high and asked if cocaine was going to get me to the big plans she somehow knew I had. Valentine's Day 2011 in a courtroom where a pen scratched out the final math on my first marriage while I was already planning which website I'd visit to numb the shame. A corporate hallway where I risked my career for thirty seconds of digital stimulation because my rewired brain convinced me I needed it more than my next breath. That night at 1:17 AM when I finally called Bobby instead of relapsing, my thumb hovering over his name for five seconds that changed everything.

Each moment contained the same choice you face right now: feed the addictions that diminish you or establish ones that expand you.

If you're reading this book, you probably fall into one of three categories, and I need you to know that I wrote this for all of you:

You might be the one in active addiction, whether to substances or behaviors, wondering if there's a way out that doesn't require you to become someone you're not. You've tried the traditional recovery routes with their emphasis on powerlessness and perpetual meetings, and something about that narrative doesn't fit the life you know you're meant to live.

You might be someone who loves an addict and desperately needs to understand what's happening in their brain, why your love isn't enough to save them, and how to support their recovery without losing yourself.

Or you might be someone who doesn't identify as an addict at all, but you know something's off—you can't put your phone down, you can't stop checking email, you can't stop shopping or eating or exercising or working in ways that feel increasingly compulsive and decreasingly satisfying.

Here's what I want you to understand before we go any further: your addiction isn't a moral failure or a character flaw. It's a sophisticated survival mechanism that your brain developed to manage pain, boredom, loneliness, or trauma, and it worked until it didn't. You can redirect the same neurological machinery that trapped you in destructive patterns toward habits and behaviors that actually serve your life if you understand how the system works and stop fighting unwinnable battles.

Back at the hibachi table, the chef catches an egg in his hat while my daughter rolls her eyes and laughs, and her laugh lands exactly where the old urgent need used to live. This is what I've learned after decades of addiction and recovery: habits are grooves worn into your neural pathways through repetition and reward, and you can't think yourself out of a groove any more than you can think yourself out of a river. Lay a new channel alongside the old one, deeper and more interesting, until the water naturally changes course.

When I aimed my addictive machinery at escape—through cocaine, pornography, and endless digital distractions—I got a counterfeit connection, a private universe of shame, and a life spent paying compound interest on moments I'd abandoned. When I learned to aim that same machinery at the right things—genuine presence with my daughters, vulnerable connection with other men, and service to fathers navigating divorce—I started craving what actually made me more alive. The machinery didn't change; the target did.

This book will teach you how to become addicted to the right things *on purpose.*

In Part I, we'll lift the hood on your neurological machinery—dopamine, trauma bonding, habit loops—so you can see exactly how your system works and why willpower alone will never be enough.

Part II will tell you the truth about what your misaimed addictions are actually costing you—not to shame you but to help you make an informed decision about whether the price is worth paying.

Part III will show you how to redirect your addictive capacity toward relationships, practices, and purposes that compound into a life worth living.

Part IV will give you the cognitive tools and high-performance habits that make your transformation sustainable, because recovery isn't about perfect days but about what you do when perfection fails.

This work is a culmination of several parts of my life. My addiction story. It's also sharing with you from study in many areas of growth and recovery. I also want to teach you how to model this alchemy in your own life, work, relationships, and journey.

In many areas, I will share directly from a source I found helpful, outlining their work, their ideas, and how that impacted my own experience. In other ways, I will summarize a combination of many things I've read, heard, or seen that has helped me create a process that I share with you here. I've compiled a listing of those sources at the end of this book if you want to research further.

Throughout it all, we'll work in five-second increments and honest inches, because that's how genuine change happens—not through dramatic gestures but through small, consistent choices that compound into identity change. We'll keep receipts instead of making vague promises, tracking what actually works rather than what sounds good in meetings.

My father's wisdom threads through every page of this book: it truly is easier to establish a new habit than to break an old one, which is why we'll focus on building before dismantling, on becoming addicted to what serves you rather than just abstaining from what doesn't.

The chef lights one final flame that reaches toward the ceiling while my phone buzzes again beneath my napkin, but I don't reach for it because I'm reaching for something better—my daughter's question about dessert and the ordinary joy of being fully present in this moment.

If you're here, you're ready for something different from the recovery narrative you've been sold, ready to stop fighting your nature and start directing it, ready to discover that the very intensity that made you an addict will make you exceptional once you aim it at the right targets.

Welcome to the truth about addiction that nobody else will tell you.

This book is meant to be used, not just read.

If you'd like support integrating the ideas as you move through the chapters, scan the QR code below to access a **free companion guidebook** created to use alongside this book. It's part of the BetterIn3.com community.

Inside you'll find:

- Guided reflections
- Simple practices
- Exercises to help you apply the material in real time

There's no right pace and no pressure to do it all.

Use what's helpful. Skip what isn't. Come back when you're ready.

PART I

Understand This: Addiction is Human, Predictable, and Trainable

The Universal Addict

If you have a brain, you have addictions. The question isn't whether—it's to what.

Standing in the checkout line at Whole Foods with four items and a restless mind, I watch my thumb unlock my phone before I've consciously decided to check it. The familiar icon pulses with its engineered promise of novelty, and my finger traces the path it knows by heart to the app that delivers a thousand tiny hits of something that feels almost like satisfaction but never quite arrives. I meant to check my calendar, but my brain had other plans, plans it made without consulting me, plans written in neural pathways carved by ten thousand previous surrenders to this exact moment.

This is the loop that runs all of us, whether we're reaching for cocaine or Instagram, pornography or Pringles, work emails at midnight or wine at noon. The machinery is identical: cue leads to craving, craving triggers ritual, ritual delivers reward, and reward teaches the brain to repeat the cycle faster next time. It's not a moral failing when you can't resist—it's your brain doing exactly what evolution designed it to do, seeking patterns and shortcuts to dopamine in a world that's learned to hack our reward systems for profit.

Let me show you how early this programming starts.

Third grade, Mrs. Carter's classroom, where the air tastes like pencil shavings and chalk dust floats through afternoon sunbeams like visible thoughts. We have to read a chapter and write a report, and I want the 'A' without the effort because effort feels like exposure, like the possibility of trying hard and still failing. So I perfected a system: skim the first and last sentences of each page, scan for bolded words and character names, then construct a report that sounds like understanding without the inconvenience of actual comprehension.

When Mrs. Carter calls for volunteers, my hand shoots up first because confidence is the best camouflage for shortcuts. I deliver my counterfeit insights with practiced enthusiasm, watching her eyebrows lift at a clever turn of phrase I've stolen from the book jacket, feeling the warm bloom of approval spread through my chest as she says "excellent work" and my classmates turn to look at me with something approaching admiration.

After the bell rings and the classroom empties for recess, she asks me to stay behind, and the silence that follows the door's click contains everything I've been running from.

"I'm proud of your writing," she says, sitting on the edge of her desk in the way teachers do when they're about to deliver truth wrapped in kindness. "You have a gift with words, and you found all the bones of the story." She pauses, letting me feel the setup before the pivot. "But you missed the muscle, didn't you? You missed what truly matters because you were so focused on appearing smart that you forgot to actually learn."

The heat rushing up my neck isn't just embarrassment—it's recognition. She's identified the loop I'm already running at eight years old: when I feel inadequate, I perform competence; when I fear being ordinary, I manufacture extraordinariness; when effort threatens to reveal my limitations, I choose the clever shortcut that preserves the illusion of effortlessness.

"Next time," she says with a gentleness that makes it worse, "do the actual work, because you're capable of so much more than clever summaries of things you haven't really experienced."

That moment contained my first conscious encounter with the machinery of addiction: the cue of potential inadequacy, the craving for approval and relief, the ritual of the artful dodge, the reward of praise without effort, and most importantly, the learning that encoded this pattern deep in my neural architecture—when you feel exposed, perform; when you fear failure, fake success; when authenticity threatens, choose the interesting lie.

This loop doesn't look like substance abuse, but it operates on identical principles and would eventually lead me to substances that could deliver the same escape more efficiently. Your brain doesn't distinguish between behavioral and chemical addictions because neurons don't care about categories—they only care about results. Whether you're chasing approval, alcohol, or achievement, the dopamine pathway lights up the same way, marking certain behaviors as essential for survival even when they're slowly killing you.

Here's what's actually happening in your brain when you run these loops, and understanding this will change how you think about every compulsive behavior in your life:

Your brain is a prediction machine, constantly calculating which actions will deliver rewards and updating its algorithms based on results. Dopamine isn't the pleasure chemical everyone thinks it is—it's the anticipation chemical, the wanting chemical, the "pay attention, this might be important" chemical. It spikes not when you get the thing you want but in the milliseconds before, when your brain recognizes the cue that signals the reward is coming. That's why the moment before you open Instagram feels more electric than actually scrolling, why the walk to the refrigerator holds more charge than the food itself, why the anticipation of the porn site delivers more dopamine than the orgasm ever will.

This anticipatory spike is also why some addictions grip harder than others, particularly those engineered by Silicon Valley's best behavioral psychologists, who understand your neural wiring better than you do. They've weaponized intermittent reinforcement—the most powerful mechanism for creating compulsive behavior—by designing feeds that sometimes deliver gold but mostly serve gravel, keeping you pulling the lever because "maybe the next one" is more interesting than guaranteed rewards. Add infinite scroll, auto-play, push notifications, and social comparison, and you've got a delivery system more sophisticated than any drug dealer could dream of, one that lives in your pocket and never runs out of product.

But the loops that really own us, the ones that reshape our lives around their demands, are those that start with pain. When you pair relief with a ritual—scrolling to escape loneliness, shopping to numb anxiety, porn to avoid intimacy, work to flee from family tensions—your brain learns something more powerful than pleasure-seeking. It learns that this specific behavior stops the hurt right now, and stopping hurt trumps seeking pleasure every time in your brain's hierarchy of needs.

This is negative reinforcement, not positive, and it's far more addictive because you're not chasing a high but fleeing a low. The relief is real and immediate even though the costs compound invisibly until they suddenly don't, until you're forty-three and your wife is standing in a restaurant parking lot looking at your phone screen with eyes that will never see you the same way again.

Here's the liberating truth hidden in this mechanical understanding: if it's predictable, it's trainable. You don't have to hate yourself to change or willpower your way to freedom. See your loops clearly, understand their function, and systematically replace them with alternatives that meet the same needs with fewer costs.

Let me give you something practical you can do right now, because insight without action is just sophisticated suffering:

Choose one loop you run regularly—maybe it's the midnight scroll when you can't sleep, maybe it's the third glass of wine when the kids finally go quiet, maybe it's the Amazon cart that fills itself when you're anxious. Map it completely: identify the cue (time, location, emotional state), name the craving (what you're really seeking—relief, stimulation, escape), describe your ritual (which app, which steps, which lies you tell yourself), notice the actual reward versus the promised one, and then track the learning—what tomorrow-you will inherit from tonight's choice.

Now here is the crucial step everyone skips: instead of trying to eliminate the loop through willpower, design a replacement that serves the same emotional function with less collateral damage. If you scroll at midnight because you're lonely, text one honest sentence to a friend about how you're really doing. To decompress, consider five minutes of breathing exercises, which calm the nervous system without liver damage. If you shop to feel in control, organize one drawer with tactical precision.

You're not white-knuckling a "no"—you're establishing a new "yes" that's more aligned with who you're becoming. This is what my father meant when he said that it's easier to establish a new habit than break an old one: you can't destroy neural pathways through resistance, but you can build stronger ones alongside them until the old ones atrophy from disuse.

The checkout line moves forward, and the cashier says hello. I look up from my phone, make eye contact, and put the device away—not because I'm virtuous but because I'm practicing a different loop, one where human connection trumps digital distraction, where presence pays higher dividends than pixels. It's not heroic; it's mechanical. Five seconds to notice the cue, one honest inch toward the life I actually want.

We all have addictions because we all have brains designed to seek patterns, avoid pain, and pursue rewards with ruthless efficiency. The question isn't whether you're an addict—you are, neurologically and behaviorally, whether your drug is cocaine or LinkedIn likes. The question is whether your addictions are aimed at targets that expand your life or ones that steadily erode it, whether you're unconsciously running loops that were programmed by your pain or consciously designing ones that serve your purpose.

In the next chapter, we'll go deeper into the chemistry that writes these loops, understanding why dopamine makes certain behaviors feel like oxygen when you're drowning, how tolerance ensures that what worked yesterday won't work tomorrow, and why the stranger in that Chattanooga bar who asked about my "big plans" understood something about addiction that most recovery programs still don't—that the solution isn't to become someone who doesn't have addictions but to become someone whose addictions are aimed at the right things.

CHAPTER 2

The Brain and Body on Addiction

Your urges aren't orders—they're predictions your brain made based on what worked before, and understanding this changes everything.

The night I learned this lesson, Depeche Mode's "Policy of Truth" was threading through the smoke and conversation of a house party in 1990, though I can't swear the song was actually playing or if my brain just assigned it later as the soundtrack to that flavor of want. I recognize the irony of that mental loop now: a song about honesty's consequences became the permanent backing track to a life built on chemical lies. Whether it was real or retroactively inserted, that synth line might as well have been my pulse, marking time between who I was and who I was about to become.

What I couldn't name then but understand with painful clarity now is that the body has a universal signature for wanting, regardless of what you're wanting. Your heart rate climbs like someone's gradually turning up the volume, your breathing goes shallow as if you're trying not to be noticed by your own conscience, your vision tunnels until the object of desire is the only thing in focus, and there's that distinctive forward pull—like someone's leaning on your sternum from the inside, pushing you toward the thing that promises to change how you feel. This surge appears identically whether you're about to snort a line, open a porn site, check your phone for the hundredth time, or eat something you swore you wouldn't—same drug, different dealer, identical neurological signature.

Freeze that moment right there, in the seconds before you surrender.

That surge you feel isn't pleasure—it's dopamine doing its actual job, which isn't to make you happy but to make you move. Dopamine is evolution's highlighter pen, marking certain cues as important enough to override your executive function, to make you forget your promises to yourself, to narrow your world to this one urgent need. It spikes not when you get the thing but when you recognize the signal that the thing is available—the notification sound, the wine bottle's shape, the familiar route past the dealer's house, the privacy of an empty home. Therefore, the five seconds before you give in can feel like fighting gravity, while the five minutes after often feel flat, disappointing, already tinged with regret.

This distinction between wanting and liking is crucial to understand if you're going to redirect your addictions rather than just white-knuckle resist them. You can want something desperately that you don't even like anymore, and many of us are trapped in exactly that loop—craving experiences that stopped delivering satisfaction years ago but that our brains still mark as essential because the pathway is so deeply carved. Your brain doesn't care about your happiness; it cares about efficiency, and nothing is more efficient than a well-worn neural highway to a guaranteed state change.

Once you understand that your brain is simply a prediction machine doing its job, you can stop moralizing your urges and start working with your neurology instead of against it.

Your brain tracks every sequence of cue-behavior-outcome, updating its algorithms based on results, strengthening the connections that delivered rewards and weakening the ones that didn't. When an outcome exceeds expectations—when the high is higher, the relief more complete, the escape more total than expected—dopamine floods the system, essentially telling your brain "whatever just happened, make sure we can do that again, faster next time." This is learning at its most fundamental level, and repetition carves these lessons into your neural architecture until they become as automatic as breathing.

This is also why the machinery of addiction is surprisingly flexible in its fuel source. When you "quit" one addiction without addressing the underlying neural patterns, your brain simply reroutes the same needs through different channels. Stop drinking and suddenly you're working sixteen-hour days; quit porn and find yourself lost in social media for hours; give up cocaine and discover online shopping delivers a similar hit. The body's anticipatory signature gives you away—the same heat in your cheeks, the same hand reaching for your pocket, the same narrowing of attention that preceded your old behavior now precedes the new one. You can feel yourself moving toward the behavior before you've consciously decided, because the decision is being made in parts of your brain that don't speak in words.

Here's where the trap gets vicious: tolerance and sensitization work in opposite directions to ensure you're never satisfied.

Tolerance means you need more of the stimulus to get the same effect— more cocaine for the same high, more extreme pornography for the same arousal, more likes for the same validation. Your brain adapts to protect you from overstimulation, but that protection becomes its own prison as you chase a satisfaction that keeps retreating. Meanwhile, sensitization means that the cues that trigger your craving get louder and more insistent. You become more triggered by less while simultaneously getting less pleasure when you give in—maximum craving meeting minimum satisfaction, the perfect recipe for compulsive behavior that feels increasingly hollow.

Novelty is the wild card that keeps this whole system spinning, because new stimuli temporarily reset your dopamine response and break through tolerance. This is why addictions escalate rather than plateau— why you need not just more but different, not just porn but new categories, not just shopping but different sites, not just food but foods you haven't tried. Tech companies have weaponized this through infinite scroll, auto-play, and recommendation algorithms that promise the next thing might be the one that finally satisfies. "Maybe the next one" isn't personal weakness; it's a design pattern engineered to exploit how your brain responds to novelty.

But here's what nobody tells you: the same machinery that traps you can free you if you learn to aim it properly.

In 2020, during the lockdown's enforced stillness, I lost 86 pounds by redirecting my addictive capacity toward fitness rather than trying to eliminate it entirely. When life lurched back toward normal and 34 pounds crept back, I didn't try to willpower my way thin—I invested in infrastructure that would make the healthy choice the simple choice. I hired a trainer not because I needed someone to yell at me but because I needed accountability that existed outside my head. Then I built a complete gym in my garage, spending money I would have once spent on my addictions on equipment that would serve my transformation.

Now, nearly every morning, I walk into that garage and feel the same anticipatory surge I once felt before using—heart rate climbing, focus narrowing, that forward pull in my chest. But now it's aimed at iron instead of escape. The playlists include Depeche Mode because I'm not trying to delete my past but to repurpose its soundtracks. On days I skip, I feel the absence not as guilt but as a genuine craving for the state change that training provides. The machinery hasn't changed; the target has.

This transformation was possible because I understood oxytocin's role in addiction, which is quieter than dopamine's but equally powerful. Oxytocin is the bonding chemical, released through repetition plus meaning plus witness, and it's what transforms a behavior from something you do into part of who you are. The ritual of training, my trainer's weekly check-ins, the photos documenting small victories, the quiet prayer before heavy sets—these aren't just habits but identity anchors that say "I am someone who trains" as surely as my old behaviors once said "I am someone who uses."

None of this means urges disappear—it means you learn to work with them strategically.

Your brain makes predictions based on context, which is why certain rooms make your palms sweat, certain times of day feel dangerous, certain songs transport you instantly to states you thought you'd left behind. State-dependent memory means that environments embed your triggers, which is why access friction matters more than motivation. If your trigger app lives on your home screen, your brain will use it like water finding the path of least resistance. Your brain will choose that path if your gym is three steps from your kitchen and you've already laid out your workout clothes.

So here's your practical prescription for rewiring your predictive machinery—what I call the Dopamine Budget, though it's less spreadsheet and more strategic sequence:

First, front-load natural rewards before noon. Stack two or three clean wins early: ten minutes of sunlight and movement, actual food and adequate water, a focused 25-minute deep work sprint on something meaningful, a genuine connection with someone you care about. Give your brain legitimate highs early so it doesn't go desperately hunting for synthetic ones later.

Second, gate artificial dopamine behind real accomplishment. If you're going to scroll social media, do it after you've created something, not as procrastination. Don't use sugar to deal with the 3 PM despair, but save it for dinner. If you're negotiating with behaviors like pornography, that conversation needs to happen in daylight with accountability, not in isolation with shame.

Third, add friction where you're vulnerable. Gray scale your phone to make it less visually addictive, use app locks that require you to pause before entering, keep devices out of bedrooms and bathrooms, change your routes during trigger windows. These barriers won't stop you if you're determined, but they'll slow you down enough for consciousness to catch up with compulsion.

Fourth, inject novelty into healthy patterns. Rotate workouts to keep your brain engaged, change playlists to prevent habituation, take different walking routes, add minor challenges you can win. You're giving your brain the "maybe this time" excitement in contexts that build rather than erode you.

Fifth, keep receipts instead of making resolutions. Each night, write one or two sentences: "Because I front-loaded exercise and sunlight, my afternoon cravings were manageable" or "Skipped morning routine, felt the pull by noon, tomorrow I anchor first." You're tracking what actually works, not what should work.

Run this system for one day and notice what shifts. Often, the urge that feels like a direct order from your nervous system softens to a suggestion you can negotiate with. The five-second window between cue and response widens enough for you to remember who you're becoming. You can hear yourself think, and thinking creates choice.

This chapter isn't about excusing your behavior—it's about understanding it precisely enough to change it. When you know that dopamine highlights while oxytocin bonds, that tolerance blunts while sensitization amplifies, that novelty seduces while context triggers, you stop fighting an invisible enemy and start engineering visible solutions. The surge in your body stops being a verdict and becomes simply information: something is about to change. The only question is whether you'll direct that change or let it direct you.

Because soon—much sooner than you think—someone you've never met will look straight through your carefully constructed facade and ask whether your current loops can carry you toward the big plans they somehow know you have. When that moment comes, you'll want your life to be the answer, not just your words.

CHAPTER 3

Short-Form and the State-Change Escape Hatch

Short-form video isn't entertainment—it's an escalator designed never to let you off.

I tell myself I'm stepping on for a single floor, sixty seconds at most, just a quick break from the tedium of waiting or working or existing in the space between meaningful moments. The feed greets me with its engineered promise of novelty, the soft haptic tick confirming I've contacted the machine that knows me better than I know myself, and the stairs begin their endless climb without asking permission. The clock on the wall says I've been here two minutes, but the clock on my phone— the one that actually tracks these things—says twenty-three minutes have evaporated into the algorithm's embrace.

Let me show you exactly what's happening in those stolen minutes.

The loop runs with mechanical precision: a small seam opens in your day—you're bored, tired, vaguely deflated by something you can't quite name—and your device sits within reach, its blue-white icon pulsing in your peripheral vision like a tiny lighthouse calling ships to rocks. The craving isn't really for the app itself but for what it promises: state change, novelty, temporary elevation from whatever emotional frequency you're stuck on. Your thumb moves through the ritual before consciousness catches up—unlock, open, flick—while auto-play eliminates the burden of choice and infinite scroll removes any natural stopping point. The rewards arrive in micro-doses perfectly calibrated to keep you engaged but never satisfied: a laugh that lasts three seconds, outrage that spikes your cortisol just enough to feel alive, a moment of awe that dissolves before you can grab it. Your brain updates its programming with each swipe: when you feel empty, this fills you; when you feel nothing, this makes you feel something; when you're stuck, this moves you. Do it again, faster next time.

The machinery works exactly as designed because people who understand your neural wiring better than you do built it. Variable rewards train your prediction engine more effectively than consistent ones—"maybe the next video" keeps you scrolling the same way "maybe the next pull" keeps gamblers at slots. The algorithm observes your every pause and swipe, creates a model of your desires, and reflects them back, referring to this curated manipulation as "personalization."

None of this makes you weak—it makes you human in a casino specifically designed for minds like yours.

Standing in that same checkout line from Chapter 1, I feel the familiar tug again, but this time I catch the full stack of cues as they assemble into compulsion: the slight sag in my chest from a morning of difficult conversations, the phone already in my palm because I just used it to pay, the tiny red notification badge promising something is waiting for me, something that might be important, probably isn't, but could change everything. My body has already started moving toward the behavior, that anticipatory lean forward, the thumb hovering over the icon, the narrowing of attention that precedes surrender.

Instead, I place the phone face down and breathe—in through the nose for four counts, out through the mouth for eight. The long exhale activates the parasympathetic nervous system, literally applying the brakes to the sympathetic acceleration that drives impulsive behavior. Ninety seconds is all it takes for the micro-urge to crest and recede like a wave that looked bigger than it was. The conveyor belt hums forward, the cashier says hello, and I'm back in the actual moment instead of the algorithmic one. This isn't heroism; it's trainability. I've added just enough friction and provided an alternative ritual that meets the same need for state change without the same cost.

Night is where the real battle happens.

The Midnight Slide always starts with the same lie dressed as a reasonable compromise: "I'll just check for a second." The room is dark except for the blue-white rectangle casting shadows across the sheets and illuminating my face from below like a campfire story told in reverse. I'm on my back, neck craned at an angle that will hurt tomorrow, eyes locked to the screen with the intensity of a predator watching prey, though I'm the one being hunted. In the darkness, novelty feels amplified, each video's audio embedding itself in my consciousness like a song you can't stop humming. Ten minutes pass, then twenty, then forty. One video triggers envy at someone's perfect life, another manufactures outrage at an injustice I can't fix, another numbs me with its meaninglessness—but each emotional spike, regardless of flavor, propels me forward because any strong feeling beats the emptiness I'm trying not to acknowledge.

The costs are quiet but compound with interest. My sleep shifts later and fragments when it finally comes, the blue light having told my pineal gland that it's still daytime. I wake with a cognitive fog that steals precision from my work and patience from my family. I snap at my daughter over something trivial and watch her face fall, and I know exactly which midnight bargain I'm paying for with her disappointment. The algorithm got my attention for free last night; this morning, everyone I love pays the price.

This isn't about shame—it's about accountability. Short-form delivers reliable state change on demand, but it collects a tax that compounds daily. The question isn't whether to use it but how to use it without allowing it to use you.

The solution isn't abstinence but architecture. You pre-decide your exits and build off-ramps that satisfy the same craving with less collateral damage.

Same bed, different night, different outcome. The phone charger now lives in another room, not because I've become virtuous but because I don't trust escalators that never stop and I'm tired of paying tomorrow for tonight's empty calories. I've placed a warm-bulb lamp across the room—if I need to get up, I'm greeted by human light instead of screen glow. The plan is simple and written where I can see it: after 10:30 PM, if the urge hits, I run a two-minute exit protocol before touching any screen.

The pull arrives on schedule, that familiar restlessness that says, "You need something," and I start with breathing: four counts in, eight counts out, three rounds. My heart rate drops from anxiety to calm. I text one friend, "Tell me one good thing from today," and wait for their response, creating connection instead of consuming content. I reach for the paper book on my nightstand and read exactly one page, not for the information but for the rhythm of real sentences written by someone who thought about them. Lights out. The urge doesn't vanish—it passes through me like weather I don't have to follow. Morning arrives with my cognitive edge intact and my emotional fuse unburned.

Here's why this works and why the tech companies hope you never figure it out.

Short-form video's architecture relies on four pillars to hack your reward system: variable rewards that train behavior faster than consistent ones, novelty density that delivers more surprise per minute than any other medium, minimal friction design that removes every barrier to continuation, and social proof that makes you feel simultaneously connected and inadequate. Your brain learns rapidly in this environment, but learning is value-neutral—you can train it toward or away from any behavior if you understand the mechanism.

When you pair your craving for state change with a pre-planned alternative that takes just two minutes, you're offering your prediction engine a different path to the same destination. Repeat this enough times and your brain expects the alternative instead of the default. You're not fighting your nature; you're redirecting it.

Design your exits and your devices like an engineer who knows the system:

Build a Two-Minute Exit Menu — six tiny interventions you can deploy in the danger zone:

- Ten slow breaths with extended exhales (inhaling for 4, exhaling for 8) to calm your system physiologically.
- Text a friend one specific good thing from your day to create an actual connection.

- 60-second wall sit or 20 squats to change your state of movement.
- Drink a full glass of water and step outside for 60 seconds.
- Read one page of a physical book to engage with crafted rather than generated content.
- Write tomorrow's single most important task on a sticky note to redirect toward purpose.

Restructure your device architecture:

- Banish trigger apps from your home screen and bury them three folders deep.
- Enable gray scale to make your phone less visually addictive.
- Disable all notifications except calls and texts from people who matter.
- Use web versions with ad blockers instead of apps when possible.
- Set sessions with boundaries: 15 minutes maximum with a specific purpose (find one useful idea, answer one question, send one message).
- Remove chargers from bedrooms and buy an actual alarm clock.
- Script your danger zones: "If it's past 10:30 PM and I feel the pull, I do one exit menu item before any screen".

Keep three receipts each night:

- Did I use an exit instead of defaulting once?
- Did I respect a session boundary once?
- Did I protect my sleep threshold?

Score yourself 0-3 and write one sentence: "Because I did X, Y improved" or "Skipped X, paid for it with Y." You're tracking what actually works, not what should work.

This isn't about becoming someone who never uses short-form—it's about becoming someone who uses it intentionally rather than compulsively. You're putting finish lines back into an arena that removed them on purpose, swapping the endless escalator for stairs you can climb with intention and stop when you choose.

Some nights you'll ride the escalator anyway because you're human and tired and the algorithm knows exactly which buttons to push when your defenses are down. Fine. Keep the receipt, adjust the protocol, and try again tomorrow. Inches compound into identity.

I keep a photo on my phone of me with my daughters laughing outside a restaurant a few days after I informed them about my second divorce. Our faces in our family traditional 'silly face' pose, building a memory that is filled with joy today, on a day that was anything but. On nights I protect my sleep boundary, I'm significantly more likely to earn that memory tomorrow instead of snap over spilled juice. That's the only algorithm I care about optimizing.

The feeds are selling you novelty at the cost of presence. But there's another escape hatch with better marketing, one that disguises numbing as nobility—when productivity becomes the drug that delivers the same empty high with a better reputation. That's where we're headed next.

CHAPTER 4

Tired Scrolling: Short-Form Video and State Escapes

When you're bored, your phone knows it before you do.

The pattern is so predictable I could set my watch to it: sitting at my desk after reading an email that deflates something in my chest, sprawled on the couch in that dead zone between dinner and bedtime, lying in bed with a day that's technically over but a brain that won't stop running its loops. The inner weather is always some variation of the same forecast—tired, vaguely sad or discouraged—and my thumb has already started moving toward the solution before I've consciously identified the problem. I promise myself just a minute, maybe two, a quick hit of something different to change the channel in my head. The feed greets me with its practiced seduction of novelty, auto-play takes over before I can form an intention, and time becomes negotiable in a way it never is when I'm doing something that matters.

Let me show you three specific ways this loop runs, because you'll recognize at least one:

The Office Drift happens after something goes wrong but not wrong enough to address directly. A proposal gets rejected, a meeting ends badly, an email arrives with that tone that means someone's disappointed but won't say it outright. Slack goes quiet, which somehow feels worse than being busy. I don't want entertainment—I want relief from this specific frequency of deflation that's not quite sadness but next to it. My thumb knows the path: unlock, open, flick. The first video delivers a small laugh, the second triggers mild outrage about something I'll forget in an hour, the third soothes through pure distraction from whatever I was feeling. Infinite scroll has removed all the natural stopping points, auto-play ensures I never have to decide to continue, and variable rewards whisper their eternal promise that the next one might be the one that actually satisfies. Ten minutes evaporate, but the actual cost comes when I try to return to work. There's an attention residue that clings to everything, like trying to think clearly through frosted glass. The problem I was avoiding hasn't gotten smaller—I've just made reentry harder and given tomorrow's version of the same problem a head start.

The Couch Doom-Scroll arrives when the dishes are done, the kids are in bed, and my bones feel too heavy to do anything meaningful but too restless to do nothing. I sink into the cushions and scroll myself into cycles of outrage and envy, watching strangers win at life while I decompose into furniture. Social proof flashes constantly—view counts, likes, transformations, victories—while the algorithm watches what makes me pause and feeds me more of the same, calling this mirror of my worst impulses "personalization." Someone's highlight reel lands like a verdict on my ordinary evening. Everyone else seems to build empires while I'm barely maintaining a household. My mood drops in perfect inverse proportion to the time spent scrolling. My sleep window shrinks, which means tomorrow's patience will too, which means tomorrow night I'll be back here, more depleted, needing an even stronger hit of escape.

The Midnight Slide is the one that costs the most because it steals from tomorrow's clarity. The room was dark except for the blue-white rectangle illuminating my face from below, turning my forearms into the only landscape that matters. In the darkness, novelty feels amplified, each video's audio threading into my consciousness like a song that will play uninvited tomorrow. I'm scrolling to avoid something—the emptiness that comes after everyone's asleep, the ache of something unfinished or unstarted, the day's collection of small failures that feel larger at night. Relief arrives on schedule, lasting exactly as long as I keep scrolling. The bill comes due at 7 AM when my alarm goes off and I'm already in cognitive deficit, trying to parent and work through the fog of borrowed time.

Here's the brutal math of short-form video: the reward isn't joy—it's relief, and relief from negative feelings is more addictive than pursuit of positive ones.

When boredom, fatigue, sadness, or discouragement become unbearable, we'll reach for any ritual that promises state change, and nothing changes states faster than a feed designed by behavioral psychologists who've weaponized every principle of conditioning. The loop learns quickly that this specific behavior delivers relief, and over time, smaller and smaller dips in mood trigger bigger and bigger pulls toward the screen. You're not chasing happiness; you're fleeing discomfort, which is why the scroll never satisfies—it's medicating a symptom while the cause metastasizes.

Engineers precisely engineered the mechanics to exploit this vulnerability. Infinite scroll removes the natural bottom of the page that might prompt you to stop. Auto-play jumps every gap before you can form the thought to leave. Variable rewards—sometimes hilarious, sometimes profound, usually neither—train persistence better than consistent rewards ever could. Social comparison adds a second hook, making your actual life feel insufficient compared to everyone else's edited existence. Together, these features create a slot machine that lives in your pocket and never closes, one that gets smarter about your weaknesses every time you use it.

But here's what nobody tells you: the same feeds that steal your attention can deliver value if you drive them with intention instead of letting them drive you.

Same desk, same deflated feeling after a difficult email, but a different approach. Before I touch the phone, I set a specific mission: find one technique to improve my squat depth for tomorrow's workout. I set a timer for ten minutes and start it before opening anything. Now I'm using the feed as a search tool, not a sedative. I scroll past the spectacle and save a video of a coach showing heel elevation with a small platform. I shared it with myself with a note: "Test Friday with 2-inch plates." The timer rings. I close the app and spend sixty seconds writing what I'll actually do: add heel elevation to warm-up, test the 90/90 mobility drill he mentioned, film myself to check depth. The session paid dividends. If it hadn't—if ten minutes passed finding nothing actionable—I would have closed the app and run a two-minute exit protocol instead.

This is the Intentional Feed Protocol that transforms consumption into research:

Before opening anything, set one specific question or problem to solve. Start a timer for ten minutes—this is non-negotiable and begins before you open the app. Save or share exactly one actionable answer that you'll apply within 48 hours. After closing, spend sixty seconds writing what you learned and what you'll do with it. If no answer surfaces in ten minutes, exit immediately and run a two-minute state-change protocol that doesn't involve screens.

Your two-minute exit menu for when the feed doesn't pay:

Breathe: Four seconds in through the nose, eight seconds out through the mouth, ten rounds. This physiologically shifts you from sympathetic to parasympathetic nervous system dominance.

Move: Twenty bodyweight squats or a sixty-second wall sit. Movement changes your state faster than thought ever could.

Shift: Step outside and find the farthest point you can see, then stare at it for sixty seconds. This literally changes your focal distance and metaphorically shifts your perspective.

The first time you try this, you'll feel the pull to "just keep looking for another minute." That's the intermittent reward schedule doing exactly what it's designed to do—keeping you pulling the lever because the next pull might pay off. Your mantra becomes simple: "If no answer in ten minutes, I'm out." Ten minutes is generous for finding something useful. If it's there, it will surface. If not, your time is better spent doing than hunting.

A crucial note about negative states: Boredom, tiredness, sadness, and discouragement aren't character flaws to be medicated—they're information to be decoded. They're telling you something about what you need: rest, connection, meaning, progress. When you flip the feed from sedation to solution-finding, you honor what these feelings are actually for—data about what needs change. If you're too depleted to seek solutions, run an exit protocol and go to bed. Tomorrow's version of you is the one worth protecting.

Your receipts for today:

Run the Intentional Feed Protocol once on a factual question that matters to you. Close the app when the timer rings regardless of what you've found. If nothing useful appeared, execute one two-minute exit and write: "Because I exited, I did X instead." Track whether exiting left you in a better state than scrolling would have.

Short-form video will always offer relief on demand—that doesn't make it evil, just powerful. The same algorithm that can steal your evening can deliver solutions, techniques, even genuine connection when you aim it deliberately. The difference between consumption and utility is two minutes of planning and the discipline to stop when the timer says stop, not when the feed decides you're done.

Novelty soothes, but there's another escape with better marketing— when productivity becomes the most socially acceptable way to avoid feeling anything. Next, we'll examine how "being busy" becomes the best-dressed addiction in the room, and how to build boundaries so your ambition compounds value instead of consuming your life.

The Stranger's Question: Congruence vs Compulsion

A stranger looked through my cocaine high and handed me my future in a single sentence.

Chattanooga, 1991, a concert where the bass ran through the floorboards like a second heartbeat and bodies pressed together until individual boundaries dissolved into collective rhythm. I had done cocaine in the bathroom twenty minutes earlier, and now the lights were strobing in perfect sync with my elevated pulse, the world narrowing to this moment of chemical clarity that felt like truth but was actually just dopamine lying to me about what mattered. Then she appeared—a girl I'd never seen before, moving through the crowd with a purpose that suggested she wasn't here by accident. She stopped directly in front of me, looked into my dilated pupils like she could see the complete story they were telling, and pulled me into an embrace that lasted long enough for my heart rate to notice it wasn't a party gesture.

When she pulled back, still holding my eyes with hers, she spoke thirteen words that would echo through the next three decades of my life: "I think you have big plans. Is cocaine going to get you there?"

The heat that rushed to my face wasn't from the drugs or the crowd—it was recognition. My body wanted to move, to deflect, to laugh it off, to disappear into the mass of people, but her question created a clearing in my consciousness where two futures suddenly became visible. One path promised immediate relief, the familiar narrowing of attention that made everything else disappear, the forward pull of a ritual that had already written the next five hours of my life in white powder and borrowed confidence. The other path was quieter but drew a line from this corner of a Chattanooga venue to the man I claimed I wanted to become—the musician with something real to say, the father I might one day be, the person whose work would matter because it came from truth instead of enhancement.

Her question didn't erase my craving—it gave my craving something to answer to.

This is the difference between the anti-drug lectures we all ignored and the moment that actually changed you: she didn't shame me, inventory my failures, or list the consequences I already knew. She witnessed me—truly saw me—and asked whether my current choices could carry me toward my stated destination. It wasn't condemnation; it was an invitation to congruence, delivered with the radical kindness that believes you can handle the truth without shattering.

That five-second pause she created, that hinge moment where decision lives, would become the template for every significant choice I'd make afterward. Not because I immediately quit cocaine—I didn't—but because she'd given me a tool more powerful than willpower: a question that could ring louder than compulsion when I remembered to ask it.

"Big plans" are beautiful in conversation but meaningless in moments of choice unless they can show up as immediate action.

After that night, I wish I could tell you I never used again, that her question transformed me instantly into someone who always chose congruence over compulsion. The truth is more ordinary and therefore more useful: sometimes compulsion won, dragging me toward the familiar ritual that promised to change my state immediately. Sometimes congruence won, pulling me toward the quieter satisfaction of choices that actually served my becoming. The difference was that now I could see the negotiation happening, could feel these two desires arguing in my chest, and could occasionally choose which one to feed.

The same pattern appeared everywhere once I learned to recognize it: the midnight scroll that promised relief from insomnia but delivered exhaustion, the third drink that offered social lubrication but stole tomorrow's clarity, the work email at 10:45 PM that felt urgent but was actually avoidance dressed as productivity. In each moment, my body would surge toward the quick state change, the reliable dopamine hit, the familiar escape. And in the better moments, the image of who I was trying to become would step into the doorway of consciousness and ask her question in my voice: "Will this get you there?"

That five-second stillness between stimulus and response is where agency lives.

It's not about hating desire or white-knuckling through life pretending you don't have cravings. It's about recognizing that you have multiple desires competing for control and choosing which one you'll obey. Compulsion is a genuine desire, sharpened by repetition into something that feels like necessity: change my state now, escape this feeling immediately, give me relief at any cost. Congruence is also a genuine desire, though often quieter: move one inch toward who I'm becoming, make choices I can respect tomorrow, build something that lasts longer than this moment. When you create stillness between cue and response, you can hear both desires clearly and choose which one deserves your obedience.

What made her intervention work wasn't just the question—it was the delivery. She approached me with curiosity instead of judgment, with a belief in my capacity instead of disappointment in my choices. She held up a mirror that showed both who I was being and who I could become, and she trusted me to handle the dissonance. That's grace: the ability to deliver truth in a way that expands possibility instead of crushing spirit.

Today, thirty-three years later, her question has become my most reliable navigation tool.

When I feel the familiar pull—toward the late-night scroll, the skipped workout, the anxiety I want to bury under busywork—I've learned to pause for one breath: in for four counts, out for eight. In the created space, I ask myself her question with my voice: "I have big plans. Will this get me there?" If the answer is no, I take one honest inch toward alignment: put on my shoes and do five minutes of movement, set the phone down and pick up a book, write tomorrow's priority and close the laptop. If the answer is yes—if what I'm about to do genuinely serves my becoming—I do it with intention and a clear endpoint. Either way, I leave a receipt: "Chose X because of Y" or "Avoided X, did Y instead." These inches compound into identity.

Congruence versus compulsion isn't a moral scoreboard—it's a navigation system.

When your actions align with your claimed values, you feel a clean energy afterward, like breathing with lungs you forgot you had. When they don't, you feel the opposite—a temporary buzz followed by a hollow echo, the hangover that comes from betraying your better self. Your body knows the difference and will teach you if you listen. The exhaustion after a midnight scroll feels different from the exhaustion after a hard workout. The anxiety after procrastination tastes different from the nervousness before a worthy challenge. Your nervous system is constantly giving you feedback about whether your choices are building or eroding you.

People think values are abstract concepts you remember in a crisis, motivational posters you hang on walls, words you say but don't live. They're not. Values are tools you deploy in the five-second hinge between cue and response. "Present father" means nothing unless it can be cashed into putting your phone down when your daughter speaks. "Durable health" is just syllables unless it shows up as choosing the stairs, the salad, the earlier bedtime. "Honest work that helps" is performative unless it directs your hands toward creation instead of consumption. Values aren't what you believe—they're what you do at the moment of choice.

Here's your practical protocol for choosing congruence:

Name your big plans in one sentence each, specific enough to steer by:

- Be a father who's fully present when my kids need me.
- Build health that carries me strong into my seventies.
- Create work that genuinely serves people's growth.
- Maintain relationships based on truth rather than performance.

Preload the question: "Will this get me there?"

In the moment of urge, create five seconds of stillness with one breath: in for four, out for eight.

If the answer is no, take one honest inch toward alignment:

- Put on shoes even if you don't run.
- Pour water even if you wanted wine.
- Text "thinking of you" instead of scrolling strangers.
- Write three sentences even if the page intimidates you.
- Set the warm lamp and read one page.
- Move your phone to another room.

If the answer is yes, proceed with a defined endpoint—know what "done" looks like.

Leave a receipt: "Chose X for Y reason." Track what actually works, not what should work.

You don't win your life through grand gestures of resistance or single moments of spectacular willpower. You win it through consistent inches—small, aligned actions repeated until they become your character. That night in Chattanooga didn't save me from addiction, but it gave me a question I could use when it mattered, and, more importantly, it gave me a way to see myself as someone worth steering toward something better.

Occasionally, I drive by the bar where the concert took place. Sometimes I can still feel the bass from that concert running underneath my current life, a reminder that past and present are always in conversation. The question remains the same—"Will this get me there?"—but now I'm both the stranger and the recipient, both the intervention and the addict, both the question and the answer. Most nights, when I choose the inch toward congruence, I sleep like someone who's becoming who he claimed he wanted to be. That's a victory worth stacking.

The right question changes not just the actor but the entire performance. Next, we'll explore how other people become living guardrails—how to invite honest witnesses into your shadows, repair quickly when you fail, and let relationships hold you accountable without letting them devour you.

PART II

Impact: How Wrong-Target Addictions Erode Connection

Counterfeit Connection: Intensity Replaces Intimacy

Intensity feels like closeness—until the lights come on and you see what you've actually built.

The parking lot was too bright for midnight, sodium lamps buzzing like accusations, casting shadows that made everyone look guilty. Car doors slammed around us as other couples headed home from dinner, normal people having normal Friday nights while we stood frozen in the space between her question and my answer. The breeze carried the smell of beer and fried food from the restaurant we'd just left, where I'd performed the role of a present husband while texting someone I shouldn't have been texting under the table.

"Where were you?" she asked, and my body responded before my consciousness could intervene.

Heat flooded up my neck like an admission of guilt. My chest went rigid with the armor I didn't know I was wearing. My eyes flicked down and to the left—the universal tell of someone about to lie. The deception reflex arrived faster than thought, my mouth already forming words designed to navigate around truth: "I was just—" Just what? Just constructing another elaborate nothing to avoid something that would change everything. I could feel the sentence reaching for its familiar cover, something soft and plausible, just enough to get past this moment and into the next one where maybe she wouldn't ask questions that cornered me into choosing between comfort and honesty.

This is how counterfeit connection works: you trade truth for intensity and call it love.

When I chased intensity—through substances, illicit texts, the dopamine hit of work emails at 10:45 PM—I got the feeling of being plugged into something vital. My nervous system lit up with adrenaline and secrecy and the particular electricity that comes from living a double life. I mistook that voltage for intimacy, confused activation for connection, and then wondered why my actual relationships felt increasingly hollow, why the person sharing my bed felt further away than the strangers in my phone.

While I was building my private rollercoaster of hidden thrills, she was losing the ground beneath her feet, one withheld truth at a time.

You can watch trust die in micro-expressions if you're paying attention, which I wasn't. The hope that lights her eyes when she asks a simple question. The barely perceptible dimming when my answer doesn't quite land, when something in my tone or timing suggests careful construction rather than simple truth. Her head tilts—not aggressively, just searching for the version of reality we supposedly share, trying to reconcile what her intuition knows with what my words claim. If you've lived with someone who lies, you know that look: it's someone scanning for the seam in the story, for the thread that, when pulled, will finally make the world make sense again.

Betrayal isn't just "you did something wrong,"—it's "I can't trust my perception anymore."

When you systematically lie to someone who loves you, you're not just hiding your actions; you're dismantling their ability to navigate reality. Their body lives in a constant flinch—hypervigilant to every inconsistency, lying awake at 2 AM replaying conversations for clues, checking and rechecking facts because nothing feels solid anymore. This isn't drama or overreaction. It's the response to living with someone who's turned reality into a negotiable commodity.

Inside my head, the lie reflex operated with mechanical precision:

Trigger: Fear of conflict, shame about my choices, the possibility of real consequences.

Action: Reach for whatever story would make the uncomfortable feeling stop.

Reward: Immediate relief—her shoulders would relax, my chest would cool, the conversation would move to safer ground.

Cost: Another brick in the wall between us, another withdrawal from the trust account, another future fight planted like a seed.

The most insidious part is how normal this becomes. You tell yourself you're protecting your partner from unnecessary pain, even as your body language broadcasts the truth you're withholding. You believe your intentions are kind while your behavior trains them to doubt their own intuition. You think you're maintaining connection through careful information management, but you're actually replacing intimacy with intensity—the intensity of secrets, the intensity of almost being caught, the intensity of the eventual explosion when it all comes out.

I need to be clear about what this does to the person on the receiving end, because I didn't understand it for years.

Betrayal trauma isn't just "hurt feelings" or "disappointment." It's a nervous system injury that doesn't heal just because you apologize. When someone's reality has been repeatedly edited without their consent, their body goes into survival mode. The threat isn't just what you did—it's the ongoing manipulation of information that makes safety impossible. If what I see isn't what's real, if my partner's words don't match their actions, if my intuition is constantly invalidated, then I can't use my own senses to protect myself. In that context, panic is rational. Checking is logical. Demanding receipts is self-preservation.

The first time I tried to repair the damage, I failed spectacularly because I was still more committed to my comfort than her healing. I confessed with conditions: "Yes, I did it, but here's why it made sense at the time." I owned the action and then immediately built a case for my defense, hoping context would soften impact, that explanation would substitute for accountability. It doesn't. Context without complete ownership is gasoline on the fire of betrayal. Every "but" tells your partner that you still think the logic of your pain matters more than the fact of their injury.

What actually works is smaller, harder, and requires abandoning your ego at the door.

Another parking lot, different night, different time, last month with Kelly, same question hanging in the air between us. The familiar surge rose—heat climbing my neck, chest tightening with defensive armor, tongue already forming the first syllable of a lie—but this time I created five seconds of space. I let the lie pass through me without using it, like watching a train I chose not to board. Then I told the truth as simply as I could manage, with a period instead of a comma, with no "but" waiting to minimize what I'd done.

"I went to that site again. You're right. I lied about it earlier today when you asked."

Then I tried something revolutionary for me: I named the impact out loud, not as performance but as acknowledgment of the reality I'd created.

"This probably makes you feel like the ground is shifting, like you can't trust what I say or what you see. You're probably replaying other conversations, wondering what else I've lied about. That's on me. I panicked and reached for the cover-up because I was afraid of this conversation. Here's what I'm going to do differently. If you need space or want to verify things, I'll cooperate without arguing."

It wasn't magic. The hurt didn't evaporate. Trust didn't restore itself because I finally told the truth once. But something shifted in the space between us—not intimacy, but the possibility of safety, which has to come first. You can't build intimacy on a foundation that keeps shifting. You have to pour new concrete and let it cure.

Safety isn't a feeling you demand from someone you've betrayed—it's a pattern you demonstrate until their nervous system believes you again.

That looked like boundaries I didn't get to negotiate down or argue against. It looked like transparency agreements that made my old self squirm: phones face-up on counters, shared calendars with real-time location, complete financial visibility, no private messaging with certain people, regular check-ins where I volunteered information instead of waiting to be asked. It looked like her saying, "Here's what I need for the next ninety days," and me saying, "Okay," without launching into a presentation about my progress. It looked like doing small, boring, consistent things: showing up exactly when I said I would, sending proof without being asked, following through on Tuesday afternoon when no one was watching.

Intensity is addicted to speed—the quick hit, the rapid escalation, the immediate gratification. Repair requires rhythm—the steady beat of kept promises, the slow accumulation of trustworthy moments, the patient reconstruction of safety through repetition rather than words.

Here's your practical blueprint for moving from counterfeit to genuine connection:

The Repair Script (memorize this before you need it):

1. **Own it completely:** "I lied about X. That was wrong." (Period. No comma, no "but," no explanation yet.)
2. **Name the impact:** "This probably made you feel Y and cost you Z. You're likely wondering what else I've hidden."
3. **Brief why (description, not excuse):** "I panicked and defaulted to my old pattern of covering up. That's my issue to fix."
4. **Specific amends:** "Here's what I'll do: A) Complete transparency about X, B) Daily check-ins about Y, C) Proof of Z by Friday."
5. **Honor their needs:** "If you need space, verification, or anything else to feel safe, I'll provide it without argument."
6. **Follow through:** "I'll send you an update by Friday at 5 PM" (then actually do it).

Boundary Agreements That Actually Work:

- **Define precisely:** Behavior + Context + Duration. "No private messaging with X. If contact is required for work, it's in writing with you CC'd. This stands for 90 days minimum."
- **Design transparency:** Devices in shared spaces, calendars visible, finances open. Kill secrecy through structure, not promises.

- **Consequence clarity:** Pre-decide what happens if boundaries break. No negotiation in the moment.
- **Review rhythm:** Weekly 15-minute check-ins. Adjust based on behavior, not feelings.
- **Protected self-care:** Each person names their non-negotiables (sleep, exercise, therapy, friend time).

Write it down. Say it out loud. Then live it in small, boring, consistent ways. Boring is beautiful in repair. Boring is what traumatized nervous systems need to heal.

There's a mantra I return to when I feel the lie climbing my throat: Safety before closeness.

Don't ask for intimacy while your partner is still bleeding from your betrayal. Stop the bleeding first through consistent, verifiable action. Then, with time and boring reliability, genuine intimacy can grow— quieter than intensity, stronger than any high you've chased, and actually sustainable because it's built on shared reality instead of managed information.

Intensity will always be available, offering its quick voltage and easy counterfeit, its promise of feeling something big without doing something real. True intimacy takes longer to build and requires you to be the same person in the parking lot that you are at dinner, the same person in your messages that you are in your marriage.

But partnership alone isn't enough when your reflexes are trained to hide. Even the best intentions buckle under the weight of old patterns. Next, we'll expand the circle of accountability: the honest witnesses— sponsors, mentors, friends who know your whole story—who can spot your lies before you tell them and hold you to the person you claim you want to become.

CHAPTER 7

Invisible Recovery: Secrecy Looks Safe, Kills Connection

I learned to look clean long before I learned to be clean, and that gap nearly destroyed everything.

The morning after tasted like shame and smelled like someone else's life—cheap floral perfume fighting with chemical sweetener, old carpet that had absorbed a thousand bad decisions, the particular staleness of a room where strangers did things they'd regret. My tongue felt like I'd been licking chalk. There was lipstick smeared on my shoulder, my chest, the inside of my thigh—burgundy marks in places that could only mean one thing, evidence of activities I couldn't fully remember but my body couldn't deny. A crust of dried blood marked where the cocaine drip had been working under my nose all night. Light cut through broken blinds in accusatory stripes, the kind of light that makes every lie visible, every choice regrettable.

The girl next to me wasn't a stranger, which made it worse. Two years older than me, someone I knew well enough to despise—her manipulations, her drama, the way she collected people's weaknesses like trophies. Yet here I was, another trophy on her nightstand next to the condom wrapper and the hand mirror with its white residue lined up like an accusation. She slept on her stomach, mouth open, a thin line of drool creating a dark circle on the pillow. Her hair was matted on one side from sweat and whatever we'd done that my blackout mind had mercy enough to hide from me.

My heart performed its post-cocaine stutter—rapid, hollow, like an engine misfiring on bad fuel. The familiar trinity arrived: devastating thirst, crushing shame, and a headache tuned to a frequency only guilt could generate. The room was suffocating in its honesty—heat, skin, industrial dryer sheets failing to mask the smell of spilled beer and regret.

More evidence revealed itself as I moved: her lipstick on my neck like a brand, scratches on my back I could feel when my shirt shifted, my jeans twisted on the floor with the belt still threaded through, one sock somehow trapped inside a pant leg, the other under a chair with a broken spindle. Three cigarette burns marked the carpet like ellipses, and an overflowing ashtray held a graveyard of her lipstick-stained filters.

I performed the coward's exit—gathering clothes in silence, navigating the minefield of creaking floorboards, treating her continued sleep like a gift from a God I'd disappointed again. The bathroom door stuck halfway, swollen from moisture and neglect. My urine was the color of concentrated shame. The clouded mirror couldn't hide what I'd become, and when I turned, I saw more lipstick marks on my ribs, my hip—a map of bad decisions written in burgundy. I pressed my tongue against my teeth to test for pain—they delivered. I swished tap water and spit pink into a drain that had seen worse. The drip still coated my throat, bitter and chemical, riding the edge between nausea and craving.

Outside, Sunday morning light fell like judgment on concrete stairs that led to a parking lot where reality waited. A pothole held last night's rain and an oil-slick rainbow that seemed too beautiful for this scene. My hands shook as I found change for the payphone, and called the only person I could face telling.

My father answered like salvation always does— immediately, without conditions.

"Hey, son." His voice carried fake coffee and Sunday certainty, the sound of a life that had never included this particular hangover. He was a pastor then, probably already showered and shaved, sermon notes and research waiting on his desk.

"I messed up. I—I used. I woke up with—" The sentence died because saying her name to my pastor father felt like swallowing glass.

He didn't sigh. He didn't sermonize. I heard him breathe—inhale, hold, slow exhale—the pause of a man choosing grace over disappointment.

"Tell me where you are," he said, steady as a foundation. "I'm on my way, son. I love you."

Relief hit me like another drug—warm, immediate, comprehensive. I gave him the address, then sat on the concrete steps watching trash move in the morning breeze while I waited for rescue from a mess I'd created but couldn't clean up alone.

He pulled up in his CRX, the same one I had first found this addiction. No lecture in the car, just his hand on my shoulder at a red light and a plan already forming. By the time we got home, he'd picked out a rehab center two states away. It was spring break from school—perfect timing for a cover story.

"We'll tell everyone you're on a trip," he said, his voice careful, protective. "A retreat. Time to think about your future."

"Even Mom?" I asked. "Even—"

"If that's what you need," he said. And that became my request—don't tell Mom, don't tell my siblings. I couldn't bear their eyes, couldn't trust even them with this version of me. My father agreed, and in that moment, our pact crystallized: we fix this privately, protect the family name, protect the ministry, protect me from the eyes of people who loved me. Love braided with secrecy, safety tangled with silence.

Twelve days in rehab felt like both forever and not nearly enough.

I detoxed in a twin bed that squeaked when I turned, sweating out cocaine and shame while group leaders talked about honesty and accountability—concepts I nodded at but didn't really internalize. I was too busy crafting the story I'd tell when I got out, the testimony that would make this all make sense, the redemptive arc that would justify the secret. I did the work on the surface—attended meetings, wrote in journals, said the right things in group—but I was already planning my invisible recovery, the way I'd manage this alone once I got home.

That was the foundation stone of what would become my prison: after those twelve days, the real invisible recovery began.

Here's how invisible recovery seduces you: You make vows in the shower where no one can hear them break. You confess to God and only God, who conveniently can't text your wife when you relapse. You white-knuckle through danger zones alone, promising yourself you'll tell the truth after you fix it—after you accumulate some clean days, after you can offer redemption instead of wreckage. The logic feels noble: Why burden the people I love with my ugliness when I can bring them the edited version, the one with a redemptive arc, the testimony instead of the mess?

But while you're protecting them from your unfiltered truth, you're really protecting your image—your place in the choir, your reputation at work, your reflection in the mirror that you need to believe is getting better. You're performing reputation management and calling it consideration. You're making a deal with secrecy that feels like dignity but is actually isolation wearing a three-piece suit.

I returned to church like nothing had happened, a three piece suit covering the bruises on my soul, hymnal open to songs about mercy I desperately needed but couldn't fully receive because receiving requires being seen. The harmony felt like absolution—voices rising, organ thundering beneath us like the heartbeat of a God who forgives even this. I sang about grace while keeping my rehab stay locked in a vault only my father had the key to. I told myself the story every addict knows: God forgives, new morning, fresh start, try harder. I told myself the lie every addict believes: no one else needs to know.

Shadow recovery thrives in holy places because performance passes for repentance when the lighting is right.

I knew exactly where to stand so the congregation couldn't see my hands shake. I had mastered the earnest expression, the perfectly timed tear during the bridge, the raised hand that suggested victory while hiding defeat. I wasn't faking faith—I was weaponizing it against accountability, using it as a spiritual bypass around the human work of confession and community.

Years later, during my first and second marriages, I traded the suit for the blue glow of a browser window, but the pattern remained identical: fix it first, then maybe tell. The triggers were mundane—boredom, stress, that particular frequency of emotional static that made escape feel necessary. The ritual was precise: check she's asleep, angle the screen away, open the private browser like a door to another world where I could be someone else for thirty minutes.

The relief was surgical—immediate, complete, then instantly hollow. Afterward, my chest would feel simultaneously empty and electrified, like I'd exchanged my soul for static. I'd delete history, clear cache, hide the phone in elaborate locations, performing an entire theater of innocence. Then I'd lie next to her in our bed, listening to her breathe, and promise myself: tomorrow I'll tell her. When it's smaller. When it's past tense. When I can say "I struggled but I'm better now" instead of "I'm drowning and I need help."

Tomorrow would arrive with coffee and kisses and dinner conversation about everything except the thing that mattered most. "Protecting her" had become protecting myself from her eyes, from the disappointment I'd see there, from the collapse of the image she had of me that I needed more than I needed freedom.

Shadow recovery always collapses, usually when you need it most.

A crisis hits—someone dies, money runs out, work implodes—and your private scaffolding buckles because it's built from promises you made to yourself, with no external accountability to hold them in place. No sponsor to call at midnight. No friend who knows your patterns. No one to text the sentence that could save you: "I'm about to do the thing."

In the morning after relapse, the house is quiet, and the person you love is sleeping next to a stranger she doesn't know is a stranger. Her body knows something is wrong—not through mystical intuition but through a thousand micro-data points: the slight distance in your kiss, the half-second delay in your responses, the way you hold your phone like it contains secrets. You both get lonelier in the same bed, isolation growing between you like a tumor neither of you will name.

The cruelest part is that secrecy begins as love.

My father loved me—he was trying to protect me from consequences that felt too big. I loved my wife—I thought I was protecting her from pain she didn't deserve. But protection without transparency is just control wearing a nicer outfit. Image management and intimacy cannot coexist. You can polish your surface or you can be held in your depths, but not both. "We'll handle this privately" can be a circle of care or a tomb where oxygen runs out.

The antidote isn't exhibition—it's witness.

My Witness Map started with three concentric circles and actual names:

Peer: A recovery friend who knew the taste of the morning after, the weight of shame, the specific exhaustion of carrying secrets. Daily text thread: status, cravings, wins, near-misses. Three-word honesty that prevents disaster: "At risk now."

Professional: A therapist who understood both addiction and betrayal trauma—not just mine but my partner's. Weekly sessions where I told the unedited version and watched my shame metabolize in another person's presence without killing either of us.

Partner: A negotiated transparency agreement—what to share, when, how, with support structures for both of us. No more ambush confessions at bedtime. No more "I'll fix it first then tell you." We wrote lanes, cadence, and emergency protocols for when the ground starts tilting.

Because relapse happens—usually as a slide, not a crash—I needed a framework for disclosure that didn't create more damage:

The Relapse Disclosure Protocol:

Preconditions: Not high, not actively acting out, nervous system regulated (walk first, breathe, cold water on face). Schedule the conversation: "I need to disclose something. Can we talk this afternoon?" This prevents emotional dumping disguised as honesty.

The Structure:

1. **Facts only:** "I viewed porn last night at 11:30 PM in our bedroom, breaking our boundary agreement."
2. **Ownership:** "This was my choice. It was wrong."
3. **Impact acknowledgment:** "I know this makes you feel unsafe and betrayed. That makes sense."
4. **Immediate safety steps:** "I've moved all devices out of the bedroom, reinstalled blockers, contacted my sponsor."
5. **Support activation:** "Would you like your support person involved? I can coordinate that."
6. **Boundaries:** "If you need space or verification measures, I'll honor them."
7. **Follow-up:** "Tomorrow at 2 PM, with my therapist on video if you want, we can process questions."

It's not cinematic. It's not romantic. It builds a life instead of destroying one.

"Tell it first, don't fix it first" became my new operating system.

Fixing follows disclosure because secrecy is the relapse extender, the thing that turns a slip into a spiral. I'm not handing my partner my recovery to manage—that's what sponsors and therapists are for. I'm giving her the information she needs to make informed decisions about her own safety and our relationship's future.

Here's something I'm sad and joyful to admit: The lessons and practices I shared above I discovered in my third marriage, at the cost of the first two. It took time. Lots of time. And it cost so much more. This book is partly my acknowledgement of things done, not done, dreamed, and realized.

Sometimes I still smell that room, taste that morning, feel the weight of my father's well-intentioned protection that nearly killed me with kindness. These aren't memories I'm trying to escape—they're receipts that remind me what secrecy costs. It looked like safety but cut off oxygen. Witnesses looked like danger but gave me air.

Your assignment:

Draw three circles. Label them Peer, Professional, Partner. Put actual names in each circle. Decide what each person needs to know and when. Save a disclosure script in your phone like you'd save emergency contact information. Practice saying "I need to tell you something" out loud until your mouth knows the shape of truth.

You can perform health or you can pursue it. You can look clean or you can get clean. The gap between those choices determines whether you're building a life or managing an image. I know which one leads to that morning-after taste, and which one leads home.

Witnesses hold you accountable, but systems make accountability possible. Next, we'll build the practical architecture—the devices, schedules, boundaries and agreements that make right choices easier than wrong ones, so you're not relying on willpower when willpower is exactly what you don't have.

Work, Willpower, and the Myth of Control

I wasn't chasing pleasure in that corporate corridor—I was chasing survival, and I didn't even know it.

The boardroom doors were heavy oak that sighed like confession booth panels when they opened. Behind them, the low frequency of pre-meeting conversation—strategic laughter, numbers dressed as jokes, the particular sound of people who've already decided what they think before you speak. My slides were perfect. I was so nervous, my mouth went dry. The hallway's aggressive air conditioning made my tie feel like a noose adjusted one notch too tight. The presentation lived in my chest like something wild trying to claw its way out.

I drifted toward the alcove by the service elevator—a blind spot I'd mapped months ago, tucked between two framed photos from a charity gala where everyone looked successful and sober. My phone sat in my pocket like a loaded comfort, its weight a promise of escape. Thumb unlock, muscle memory faster than conscious thought. Blue light baptism. A quick scroll through nothing that mattered—sports scores I wouldn't remember, a message from someone I didn't care about, headlines designed to make me angry about things I couldn't control. Ten seconds of invisible relief, just enough dopamine to fool my nervous system into thinking we weren't about to die. Breath drops from throat to belly, shoulders unhunch, the wild thing in my chest goes quiet.

Footsteps. Marcus.

I shoved the phone back with the specific shame of someone caught masturbating at work. He rounded the corner carrying a folder and the unforgivable confidence of someone who exercises before dawn and drinks the recommended amount of water. His eyes tracked the alcove, tracked me, tracked my hand leaving my pocket. "You good?" The question that isn't a question. I smiled with the part of my face I could control. "Good," I said, voice pitched half a note too high, the tell of a man whose nervous system just got caught self-medicating.

He held my gaze two beats longer than comfortable—that particular pause of someone who sees your tremor but has the grace not to name it—then disappeared through the oak doors.

I followed, already scattered. The micro-hit of phone dopamine left its residue: attention fragmented, presence compromised, like trying to think clearly through frosted glass. I was processing notifications that didn't matter instead of preparing for the opening sentence that did. Slide one appeared. I heard myself speak from somewhere outside my own skull—too fast, defensive edge, that subtle hunt for approval that makes strong points sound like questions. The room's energy shifted. Questions came early, before I'd built credibility. I answered, but my voice carried the vibrato of someone whose foundation was already shaking.

I kept telling myself I could push through with willpower. I kept creating situations that required superhuman willpower to survive.

This is the myth that nearly destroyed my career: that productivity is primarily a moral quality, that strong people white-knuckle their way through dysregulation while weak people reach for their phones. The truth is less flattering and infinitely more useful. Your brain cannot produce elite work in a dysregulated state—it produces escape plans. When stakes spike and your body screams for relief, every cell in your nervous system starts hunting for the fastest state change available. If you don't provide one intentionally, it will find one in your pocket, your browser, your fantasy life, anywhere but here.

That corridor phone check wasn't giving me information or connection— it was giving me just enough dopamine to survive the next sixty seconds. My nervous system had learned to use my device as a pacifier, and then I tried to deliver a board-level presentation with pacifier residue still coating my cognition. The invoice arrived immediately: stumbled transitions, forgotten points, answers that sounded like someone driving with the parking brake on.

Let me show you two mornings that live in my memory like before-and-after photos of what's possible.

Morning A (The Old Way): Wake up already behind, phone in hand before my feet hit the floor, letting other people's urgency write the opening chapter of my day. Twenty emails before coffee, each one adding weight to my chest. I promise myself today will be different—I'll be strong, I'll focus, I won't check my phone between tasks like a lab rat hitting a lever. By 10:30 AM, I'm bargaining with myself—just two minutes of scrolling—and by lunch, my attention feels like confetti someone threw in a wind tunnel. I blame my character, my generation, my moral weakness. I promise to try harder tomorrow, which is exactly what I promised yesterday.

Morning B (The New Way): The night before, I staged everything like a surgical team preps an operating room. Phone charges in the kitchen, analog watch on the nightstand, one-sentence plan written on an index card: "Complete investor deck section 3, focus on narrative arc." Morning arrives. Before touching anything digital, I breathe for sixty seconds—four counts in, eight counts out, the physiological sigh that tells my nervous system we're safe. Phone stays docked at my office door like a coat I'm not wearing inside. Headphones on, fifty-minute timer visible, single task on screen. At the break, I stand, walk to the window, drink water, write the next concrete action. By 10:30 AM, I have real work in the bank and a nervous system that trusts me because I've kept my promises to it.

Environment beats willpower because it operates below the threshold of decision fatigue.

You can be disciplined and still lose if your default environment is designed to scatter you. I had to stop fighting my nervous system and start designing for it.

The solution wasn't becoming stronger—it was building rails that made strength unnecessary.

The Phone-Out/Focus-In Protocol emerged from pure necessity. Before any high-stakes situation:

Physical separation: Phone goes in a bag, bag goes in a drawer, drawer is in another room. Twenty seconds of friction between impulse and action—enough time for your prefrontal cortex to catch up with your limbic system.

Tool staging: Only what I need, arranged like a surgeon's instruments. Printed agenda, pen, index card with three words: "Goal: Land narrative. Pace: Measured. First question: Sarah."

Device castration: When I must have the phone, I make it boring. Grayscale on, social apps buried in folders, notifications off except for actual emergencies (hint: almost nothing is an emergency).

State preparation: Sixty seconds in that same alcove, but now I'm breathing instead of scrolling. Four counts in, eight counts out. This down-regulates your nervous system more effectively than any app ever could.

The first time I walked past that alcove with my phone locked away, the itch felt like withdrawal—because it was. My hand performed the phantom pocket-pat, that unconscious check for the digital pacifier. The corridor photos seemed to pulse with invitation. I breathed through it, told my nervous system out loud, "You're not dying, this is just a presentation about revenue projections." The urge didn't disappear—it just lost its authority over my behavior.

Inside the boardroom, I started deliberately slower. Delivered the first sentence, then shut up to let it land. When questions came, I took a breath before answering—not a dramatic pause, just enough space to think before speaking. The room leaned in instead of checking phones. Marcus's eyes did something I'd never seen—they focused completely on what I was saying.

Afterward, he caught me by the coffee machine. "Different today," he said. Not a performance review, not false praise—just a colleague acknowledging that something had shifted in how my words landed in the room.

I didn't become a hero of willpower. I became someone with better architecture.

Here's the physics that saved my career:

Friction: Make the wrong thing require effort. Distance, delay, difficulty. Twenty seconds of friction kills more urges than twenty hours of self-talk.

Fuel: Make the right thing obvious and ready. Tools visible, next action clear, progress trackable. Your future self is lazy—set everything up so they can't fail.

Rhythm: Stop expecting eight-hour marathons of focus. Work in sprints your nervous system can trust.

The 50/10 Deep Work Sprint became my new operating system:

- Fifty minutes on a single target (timer visible, inputs off, world on mute).
- Ten minutes of recovery (stand, walk, breathe, water).
- Write two sentences: what I completed, what I'll start next.
- Repeat 2-3 times.
- Leave a receipt: "Completed X, next action Y".

When the urge to check hit mid-sprint—and it always did—I wrote the word "URGE" in the margin, took two breaths, returned to the sentence. No moral judgment, no character assassination, just data collection like a scientist noting weather patterns. The act of naming the urge created just enough space to not obey it.

In teams, we made focus social without making it performative.

Shared timer on the wall. Whiteboard with names and one line each: what you're working on. Sixty-second check-ins at breaks—no speeches, no heroics, just "I'm on section three of the deck, next is financial projections." We normalized deep work as something we build together, not a private struggle we hide.

The corridor became my laboratory. Every moment of temptation was data, not evidence of deficiency. When shame flushed my face, I used it as a compass pointing to a design flaw. I didn't need more character—I needed more friction between me and my escapes.

Here's what I wish someone had told me at twenty-five, when I thought success meant feeling like you're on fire all day:

Your nervous system is not the enemy of your productivity—it's the foundation your productivity is built on. Regulate the foundation and the building stands. Try to build on quicksand and everything collapses, no matter how hard you work.

Before your next high-pressure moment, write one sentence on an index card. Put your phone somewhere that requires a small journey to retrieve. Breathe out twice as long as you breathe in. Walk past your usual escape route like someone who knows where real relief comes from. Give your brain fifty minutes of clean focus, then honor it with real rest. Document what worked.

This isn't about nobility or moral superiority. It's about what actually works when you need to perform and your nervous system wants to flee.

Systems, not sermons. Architecture, not willpower. Boring, effective, repeatable.

But architecture at your desk is one thing. Next, we'll take these rails into hostile territory—airports, hotels, conference bars—where every surface is designed to scatter your attention and every moment offers an escape. We'll build guardrails that travel, because your triggers don't stay home when you leave.

CHAPTER 9

Fatherhood, Divorce, and Distance: Love as Logistics

I measured fatherhood in miles and receipts. I measured marriage in the distance I kept. One measurement built my daughters' trust; the other destroyed my wife's.

From 2011 to 2019, our car became a family organism, expanding and contracting with the custody calendar. I had remarried—a young family with old patterns I hadn't addressed. Emmy lived in Florida with her mother. We lived in Tennessee. In September 2012, Livvie arrived—tiny hospital hat, impossibly small fingers, the sudden recalibration of everything. The trips didn't stop; they multiplied. Trunk Tetris evolved into a complex equation: pack-and-play wedged against the stroller, duffels balanced on a cooler, the soft bag with sunscreen and those googly-eyed mini golf pencils Emmy insisted were lucky, board books with corners already gummed, bottles sorted by hours until the next stop. Love as logistics scaled to fit four hearts.

The night before each run, our house transformed into command central. Car seats checked for the third time. Bottles prepped and staged. Snacks sorted by who had teeth for what. The route memorized like a prayer—I-75 south through Atlanta and west on Florida's Turnpike, each exit a bead on a rosary of arrival. The Florida line where we changed stations. The first palm tree that meant we were close. Even with a baby crying and a marriage I was secretly failing, we kept the spine of our rituals intact. Emmy wasn't a guest star in our expanded family—she was the gravity we organized around.

We saved birthdays so Emmy could be there. Even Livvie's.

This was inconvenient and perfect. We moved parties, held cakes hostage, told well-meaning relatives "No, not that weekend" because we were writing a story bigger than convenience. The year Livvie turned four, we drove the party to Florida so sisters could smear frosting on each other's faces and fight Peter Pan style - Livvie loved Pan and Emmy took the role of Hook. When candles needed to be blown out, Emmy leaned in, her breath mixing with her baby sister's, two girls becoming one wish. The photo from that day shows what we were trying to build: not a split family but a family that splits distance to stay whole.

Most of it looked like beautiful chaos. Hotel lobbies that smelled like chlorine and optimism, a stroller drying in the corner, keycard working on the third try like always. "Hello, ocean" on the first night regardless of arrival time—me carrying a sleeping baby, Emmy saying it extra loud to claim her territory in the ritual. After beach, ice cream at the same place where the teenage employee now called Livvie "assistant to the boss" while Emmy beamed at the promotion she'd granted. Photos under the flickering cone sign now showed two girls—the frame widening to hold us all.

Mini golf remained our mass. Hole seven became a growth chart for three: Emmy rising, me sinking to meet her, Livvie's stroller handle creeping into frame like a witness. Scorecards accumulated in the glove compartment—receipts with pencil smudges, applesauce fingerprints, the careful math of documented love.

We worked hard to prove Emmy wasn't forgotten.

Story time waited for her visits so she could choose Livvie's books. First aquarium trip, first successful mini golf game—delayed until she could witness them. We practiced saying "You're not an add-on, you're the reason" until it became true in our bones. Children don't believe words; they believe patterns. We turned our promises into highway miles.

The drives felt different with a full car—my wife's hand on my knee at stoplights, Livvie babbling in the back, Emmy explaining elaborate stories about her friends to an audience finally big enough to appreciate them.

The cashier with the wrist tattoo would say "Headed south?" to all of us, and my wife would laugh with her hair up and her eyes tired in that specific way that means you've packed half a house twice. We looked like a team. We performed like a team. What she didn't know was that I was keeping score in a game she didn't know we were playing.

Here's what I have to tell you: while I was building a reliable identity as a father in public, I was maintaining careful distance as a husband in private.

My porn addiction didn't care that I'd remarried. It thrived in the spaces I protected—during naps, after bedtime, on business trips, through a phone I'd learned to hide in plain sight. I could be heroic with calendars and cowardly with truth. I invested everything in rituals my daughters could see while maintaining barriers my wife could only feel. The buffer I built to "protect" everyone from my shame ended up protecting me from intimacy. I was present on schedule and absent by design.

I can list every beautiful detail from those years because they're true: bookstore runs with both girls (Emmy reading staff picks to Livvie, who grabbed at books that squeaked), Sunday pancakes in red vinyl booths (high chair pulled close, syrup distribution like a NATO negotiation), homework at hotel lobby tables (hot chocolate lids secured after The Great Math Sheet Flood), goodbye rituals (coins in shoes, dates repeated like incantations). These receipts built my identity as a father. They were good. They were necessary. They kept my daughters' nervous systems regulated across state lines.

But identity is plural, and the man who could point to a glove compartment full of scorecards was the same man with a browser history he burned.

My wife slept next to someone whose eyes drifted to screens instead of to her face, who built elaborate logistics for connection with his daughters while maintaining calculated distance from her heart. I kept showing up in the car. I kept disappearing in the marriage. Love as logistics carried my daughters and cost me my marriage to Livvie's mom.

Let me be precise about this paradox: the logistics mattered. Rituals are how children metabolize love into something their bodies can trust. "With Dad, we always..." is a sentence that builds identity when geography is cruel. We saved birthdays so sisters could know each other. We rerouted entire seasons so a girl in Florida could be the center of a family in Tennessee. That wasn't performance—that was devotion with documentation.

And also: logistics are not intimacy.

They're the rails, not the train. I built immaculate rails while refusing to board any train that would carry me closer to my wife. Distance became my most protected asset—first from shame, then from confrontation, finally from the vulnerability that real intimacy demands. I called it being strong for the kids. Sometimes it was. Often it was how I avoided being known.

There's a photo from 2015 that breaks me: game of golf with the daughters, on hole seventeen, Emmy's arm around my neck like she owns me, Livvie mid-squirm in toddler chaos, my smile real but partial—a man proud of his receipts, hiding his debt. A week later, there's an invisible photo: bathroom light at 1:12 AM, a phone I shouldn't be holding, a loop I promised to break and didn't. Both lived in the same body. Both were choosing different futures.

So what do I give you beyond confession? Tools that account for the whole man, not just the public father.

The Signature Promise + Ritual Builder (for your kids):

1. **Choose one domain:** arrival, departure, weekly call, monthly adventure.
2. **Write a promise that fits on a dashboard sticky note:**
   - "First night: ocean walk (five minutes minimum), then one scoop."
   - "Sunday pancakes, red booth, you order, we split the bacon."
   - "Airport goodbye: bridge coin, next date spoken twice."
3. **Build the logistics:** Calendar it, pack it, create backups.

4. **Track it:** Date, place, one line, one photo. Review quarterly together.
5. **Evolve the surface, keep the spine:** When they outgrow the activity, preserve the structure.

The Signature Disclosure (for your partner):

This is intimacy's version of logistics—when and how you tell the truth about your inner world, your struggles, your actual location (psychological and physical). Don't let "good father" become the costume that hides "absent husband." If there's a buffer, map it. If there's an addiction, name it to a peer, a professional, and your partner through negotiated channels. Your kids' stability cannot be the excuse for your spouse's loneliness.

Here's what those years taught me:

We kept saving birthdays so sisters could blow out candles together. We walked to the ocean with a baby sleeping on my shoulder and Emmy skipping circles around us like a protective satellite. We made hotel homework a ritual that survived three different curricula. Those receipts built something that still holds my daughters steady.

And I lost a marriage while holding those same receipts. Both are true. Both require different kinds of courage.

Love as logistics sounds cold until you're the kid waiting at the window—then it's everything: the car that arrives when promised, the person who walks through the lobby saying your dumb joke, the proof that you matter made visible through consistency.

Love as intimacy sounds risky until you're the partner lying next to a familiar stranger—then it's oxygen you didn't know you were missing.

Your assignment:

Plan, prep, show, ritual, receipt, repeat—for your kids.
Tell, disclose, draw near, repeat—for your partner.

The first loop I mastered. The second I learned too late. If I could hand you anything from those years, it's this: do both. Put the same energy you invest in birthday logistics into dismantling the buffers you've built. The same creativity you use to make hole seven magical, use to make your relationship transparent.

Rituals make love durable for children. Truth makes love possible between adults. Next, we'll build protocols for when both systems fail—when flights cancel, when disclosure goes badly, when the perfect plan meets imperfect humans. Not grand gestures or dramatic saves. Just the next right inch, documented and delivered.

PART III

Transition: From Urge Management to Healthy Addiction

CHAPTER 10

Early Recovery: Surfing Urges Without Lying

At 1:17 AM, I chose a voice over a browser. That choice saved my life.

The room had that specific post-midnight texture where silence becomes a presence—streetlight cutting stripes across the ceiling, the phone face-down on the nightstand like a loaded weapon pretending to sleep. My body was already screaming: jaw locked, chest electric, fingers twitching with that particular frequency that means I'm five seconds from a decision that will destroy tomorrow.

The bargaining committee convened instantly:
Just check the news.
You're not going to act out, you're just... looking.
You've been good for three days. You deserve some relief.
No one will know.

I rolled to the edge of the bed and let my feet find the cold floor—the first honest move. The addiction hates verticality. It wants you horizontal, scrolling, surrendering.

My thumb hovered over the square where destruction lives, muscle memory already pulling me toward the familiar spiral. Instead, I said "witness" out loud—a single word I'd practiced until it became a life raft. I opened contacts instead of Chrome and tapped Bobby's name.

Two rings. Then his voice, rough with sleep but immediately present: "Yo," the vowel stretched like he had all night.

"It's me," I said. "Wave's at an eight. Walking now."

He didn't ask for a backstory. He didn't offer platitudes about my strength. He said, "Walk with me," and I heard him shift, sheets rustling, his breath getting louder so I could match it. Four counts in. Eight counts out. I paced the hallway while he breathed me back to earth.

The cheap runner rug compressed under my feet. Kitchen tile shocked cold through my socks. I ran my wrists under the faucet for ten seconds—an old detox trick that reminds your nervous system it has edges.

"Name it," he said.

"Porn urge. Eight out of ten." Numbers make monsters manageable. Eight is high but not terminal.

"Timer," he said.

I set twelve minutes—the typical lifespan of an unchecked urge. "What's the wall color?"

"Rental beige," I said. "That specific shade of nothing landlords think is sophisticated."

"Perfect," he laughed. "Keep noticing stupid things."

We didn't excavate my childhood trauma. We didn't analyze my triggers. We didn't perform therapy. He kept me tethered to the present through mundane observation: the way streetlights made the doorframe look painted, the five ingredients on the cereal box I read aloud, the number of magnets on the refrigerator. He held his voice in that grounded frequency only available to people who've been saved and done the saving.

At minute eight, the wave crested and began its retreat. You can feel it—like taking off a backpack you forgot you were carrying. Shame wants you to believe urges are destiny. Recovery taught me they're just weather. You don't argue with rain; you find shelter.

"Where's the phone going?" he asked when he heard my breathing settle.

"Kitchen drawer. Charging. Door closed between it and me."

"Good. Text me two lines and get some sleep."

I sent the receipt: *Urge surfed. Phone docked. Alarm on analog watch.*

I returned to a bed that looked identical but felt completely different. The room still wore streetlight stripes, but I had a receipt instead of relapse residue.

Early recovery has its own physics, and my body knew the choreography from a different addiction in a different decade.

Fall 1989: my first line of cocaine at sixteen, the beginning of a spiral that would teach me everything about shame and nothing about healing. Spring 1991: seventeen years old in a detox chair, learning that cravings aren't commands, that a steady voice can lower the volume in your veins. I got clean briefly, relapsed when senior year started, carried the habit through freshman year of college like a secret tumor.

The morning after one particularly brutal binge in 1991, I woke up next to someone I actively despised—her and myself equally. Lipstick on my chest in places that proved what I couldn't remember. My father's voice on the phone: "Tell me where you are. I'm coming to get you." Twelve days in rehab, a story we told no one, not even my mother. The invisible recovery that would become my template for the next thirty years.

I finally put cocaine down in January 1993 and haven't touched it since. But sobriety from one substance doesn't mean recovery from the pattern. I simply relocated my escape routes—porn instead of powder, browser history instead of bloody tissues, the same physics with different particles: trigger, isolate, consume, shame, repeat.

My marriages became milestones in this endless loop.

Emmy's mom, 1997-2006: I could stay clean from cocaine but not from the distance I maintained through secret browsing sessions, and the lies that hiding the activity required.

Livvie's mom, 2009-2020: A decade of being heroic with custody schedules and cowardly with honesty, building elaborate logistics for my daughters while maintaining calculated distance from my wife.

The Tennessee-to-Florida runs from 2011-2019 weren't just custody trips—they were my attempt to be the father I needed to be while hiding the husband I actually was. I lost my marriage in 2020 partly because I kept a browser window between me and intimacy, calling the gap "protection."

So when I say that at 1:17 AM in 2020 I chose a voice over a browser, I'm speaking as someone who had run both patterns to their conclusion.

The call to Bobby wasn't my first attempt at recovery—it was my first attempt at recovery that included other people in real time. The difference between 1990 and 2020 wasn't the urge; it was the witness in the gap.

In 2022, I married Kelly, and with her came three more daughters—Jenna, Linda, and Laura. Our Tennessee house now holds five daughters' worth of chaos: music from three rooms simultaneously, dishes multiplying in the sink, family meetings about missing sneakers. It's the kind of beautiful mess that makes isolation both harder and more tempting—harder because witnesses are everywhere, more tempting because chaos provides cover.

Kelly and I did something my younger self would have considered impossible: we pre-negotiated honesty.

We built lanes like guardrails on a mountain road:

- No bedtime ambush confessions.
- Real-time texts for high-risk moments: "Dysregulated, not dangerous. Urge at 8. Calling Bobby. Update by 7 AM."
- Her scripted response: "Thank you for telling me. I'm here. What's your next step?"
- Separate support circles so neither carries the other alone.

The first time we ran this protocol—kids asleep, dog dreaming, me with an urge at nine—I braced for the old verdict: *Get away from me.* Instead, she touched my shoulder, stayed in her lane, let me step into mine. I called Bobby. I walked. The wave became weather. We slept in the same bed because we'd put the phone in the kitchen like a pet learning its crate.

What changed everything wasn't willpower or wisdom—it was a protocol simple enough to execute when I'm stupid with urge. It was my welcoming the Witness into the equation.

I want to share the protocol with you in a way that I hope will help you, because let's face it, addiction lives everywhere, not just in substance or porn abuse, but in everyday situations where our emotions take over and we run for what calms us down.

The Urge Surf Protocol (on an index card taped where my hand goes in the dark):

1. **Name:** Say it aloud with a number. "Porn urge: eight." Naming shrinks monsters; numbers prevent catastrophizing.
2. **Locate:** Where in your body? Jaw? Chest? Hands? Put your palm there. Notice temperature, pressure, frequency.
3. **Breathe:** Four counts in, eight counts out, one full minute. Longer exhale tells your nervous system: no tiger.
4. **Delay:** Set 12-minute timer. No new decisions until it ends. You're not quitting forever; you're waiting out the weather.
5. **Dial:** Call your pre-loaded witness (Peer, Pro, or Partner in agreed lanes). First words: "It's me. Wave high. Walking now."
6. **Document:** One small, verifiable safety action. Phone in kitchen. Barefoot on cold ground. Wrists under water. Text receipt: "Urge surfed. Phone docked. Next: sleep."

It's not heroic. It's repeatable. That's what makes it lifesaving.

There's a lie that says good people don't need midnight phone calls.

That's addiction speaking in a three-piece suit. The truth is inverted: healthy people are compulsive about connection. They turn *witness* into *reflex*. They get addicted to boring supports—sleep hygiene, meeting schedules, walking routes, breathing patterns. They practice until their thumb automatically hits a contact instead of a browser.

I still remember the first relapse disclosure in 1991 where my friend's face went cold, his voice flat: "Get away from me." My chest turned to ice. The difference in 2020 that night at 1:17 AM, I didn't have a fair-weather friend. I had Bobby. That's not betrayal—that's triage. Recovery means you stop auditioning people for roles they can't play. You no longer expect functions from friendships that aren't skilled to perform that task. You bless them and build a different circle.

Here's Your assignment:

For use when you're in crisis and feel like you're about to slip back to that *thing* that has controlled you for long enough. No matter if that thing is alcohol or Instagram.

1. Write three words on a card and tape it where your hand goes in the dark: "Call. Walk. Water." Or just two: "Witness first."
2. Pin three contacts. Label them clearly. Tell them: "If I call after midnight, I'm not asking for advice. I'm asking you to breathe with me."
3. Practice the first sentence aloud when you're calm so your mouth knows the shape when you're burning.

You're going to have nights when the addiction wins. Don't let those become solitary confinement. In the morning, tell first, fix second. Text your peer. See your professional. Put the phone back in the kitchen because you still mean it.

Track your success not in perfect days but in witness-first responses. Count waves surfed, not waves that never came. The waves will get smaller, shorter, almost boring in their predictability. The gap between urge and action will expand because your body starts trusting you.

At 1:17 AM, the ceiling still wears stripes. The phone still waits like a hungry animal. Your nervous system still wants relief. But now there's a voice on the other end of a line who knows your name and how to say it in a way that brings you home.

Choose the voice. Every time, choose the voice.

Recovery isn't about never having waves—it's about learning to surf them with witnesses. Next, we'll build the healthy addictions that make the unhealthy ones irrelevant: connection, sleep, movement, meaningful work. Cravings you can trust. Habits that love you back.

CHAPTER 11

Alone Together: Isolation as X-ray

Lockdown turned my life into an X-ray. Everything external that held me upright vanished, leaving only the fractures I'd been walking on.

The first week, my house felt like an airport at 3 AM—fluorescent and abandoned simultaneously. Commute: deleted. Office: pixels on a screen. Gym: a memory. Human faces became tiny aquariums, each person breathing behind their own glass. Noon sounded like the refrigerator humming. Two-thirty PM looked like dust particles suspended in window light. Eleven-thirty PM stretched like taffy that never snapped back. Without external architecture, I discovered how much of my integrity had been outsourced to other people's schedules and eyes.

Alone together became one endless, shapeless hour.

The browser's gravitational pull peaked at two precise moments: 2:30 PM and 11:30 PM. At 2:30, my brain went hunting for dopamine—news, feeds, anything with infinite scroll. At 11:30, the addiction whispered its favorite lie: *No one's watching.* In the before-times, a meeting would interrupt, a commute would break the spell, the gym would close. In lockdown, interruption became something I had to engineer from scratch.

I called Bobby. "My systems are dissolving."

He laughed—his particular brand of love. "Perfect. Now we can see the bones."

We opened FaceTime and turned a delivery box into a diagnostic tool. On the left side, I wrote the hours I kept failing. On the right, the locations that made it worse. No psychoanalysis. Just data. Where did I make deals with the devil? When did my energy drop below functional? What impossible tasks was I assigning to my depleted future self?

The first redesign wasn't inspirational. It was triage with compassion.

- **Phone dock relocated to the hallway at 9 PM.** Not a suggestion—a physical docking station that clicked like a seatbelt. The phone sleeps outside the bedroom, period.
- **Browser blocker from 11:30 PM to midnight.** Not forever—just long enough to survive the sharp bend in the night where I lost my name.
- **Sneakers by the door with a Post-it: "2:25 PM = 2 laps."** Movement as medication, scheduled like insulin for a diabetic.
- **Water bottle on desk, always full.** Dehydration masquerades as despair. Most existential crises are actually biological.
- **Three alarms labeled "BREATHE 90s"** at 8:30 AM, 2:25 PM, and 9:00 PM. The body needs reminders to be a body.

I couldn't trust my depleted self to remember any of this, so Bobby scrawled **NO NEW DECISIONS AFTER 9** in Sharpie across an index card we taped to my monitor. Choice becomes expensive after dark.

Day one: I hit one out of five protocols. Still crashed into the 11:30 wall, made it to 12:07 before the blocker saved me from myself. I hated it for working.

Day two: Did the 2:25 walk. Returned winded, irritated, and mysteriously clear. The light had shifted on the wall. The urge that felt like oxygen ten minutes earlier now felt optional.

Day four: Docked the phone at 9 PM. My nervous system threw a tantrum like I'd stolen its pacifier.

Day five: Slept through the night for the first time in weeks.

The improvements weren't beautiful. They were functional. But functional is how you rebuild a skeleton.

Lockdown revealed the brutal difference between external structure and internal structure.

External structure is scaffolding: the office door you walk through, the gym that closes at 10, the meeting where someone makes eye contact when you share. It's powerful because it makes virtue automatic.

Internal structure is skeleton: the rituals you execute without witnesses, the constraints that prevent your 11:30 PM self from making promises your 7 AM self can't keep. When scaffolding disappears, the skeleton either holds or collapses. Mine collapsed. Then we reinforced it.

I used to think willpower was character. Isolation taught me that **energy is the precondition for character.** Exhausted brains make terrible bargains. Low blood sugar looks exactly like moral failure. The days I slept poorly, the browser pulled like a black hole. The days I ate garbage and avoided sunlight, the five-second gap between urge and action felt like a luxury I couldn't afford.

So we started tracking energy like a bank account.

The Energy Ledger: Simple accounting for complicated humans.

Morning: List three deposits, three withdrawals.

- Deposits: Ten minutes of sunlight before screens, 25-minute walk, one call with someone who makes me laugh.
- Withdrawals: Back-to-back Zooms, custody paperwork, difficult conversation with ex.

Midday: Score the tank from 1-10. Below 5? Deploy emergency protocols immediately.

Evening: One minute to note what moved the needle. Schedule tomorrow's deposits before tomorrow's chaos.

These became my first healthy addictions—sunlight, breath, movement, witness—because they return more energy than they consume.

I discovered my energy didn't just drop; it hemorrhaged through specific leaks. Email until the bucket clanged empty. "Breaks" that were actually scroll-holes. I learned to bundle temptation with movement: phone calls only while walking, podcasts only on the rower, music only while cooking. I learned that 90 seconds of breathing—inhale four, hold two, exhale eight, hold two, three rounds—was like washing windows from the inside. Shoulders unhunch, jaw releases, attention returns from exile.

That 90 seconds bought me an hour. The hour bought me a win. The win bought me the desire to do it again.

Here's the loop we were installing: Energy creates clarity. Clarity enables action. Action produces wins. Wins return energy. Repeat until it becomes automatic.

Same physics as addiction—cue, action, reward—but aimed at health instead of harm. Once your nervous system trusts these patterns to pay dividends, it starts requesting them.

The rewards became visceral, not virtuous. The 2:25 walk left a clean burn in my legs and unexpected brightness behind my eyes. The breathing made my ribs feel properly weighted, like my body had finally found the ground. Water tasted sharp and necessary instead of like an interruption. Ten minutes of sun turned my forearms warm and the room less hostile. Small, mammalian rewards. Reliable in ways the scroll never is.

The constraints felt insulting initially—training wheels for a grown man. Then I remembered: I wasn't designing for my best self. I was designing for the version of me who emerges after five Zooms and a nasty text from a teenager, the one who wants relief more than victory. **Pre-committed compassion is what constraints actually are.**

Stress still spiked. Custody logistics during a pandemic require PhD-level mathematics. Money got weird. Loneliness did what loneliness does—turned every room into an echo chamber of self-assessment. Some nights I relapsed into old patterns, woke up with familiar shame. The difference wasn't the shame disappearing. The difference was not turning shame into a referendum on my character. We debugged the system instead of prosecuting the person. **Technical problems, not moral failures.**

"I hate that recovery is just boring rules," I told Bobby during one particularly low FaceTime.

He grinned. "Boring saves lives. Sexy got you here."

We kept building the unsexy infrastructure:

- Focus modes tied to calendar blocks.
- Whitelist-only browser after 9 PM (if it's not pre-approved, it doesn't exist).
- Two-minute voice memo to Bobby every evening: energy score plus tomorrow's plan.

"Today was a 5 at 2 PM. Walked. Helped. Tomorrow's deposits: sunlight, call Jenny, twenty minutes writing before email opens."

After weeks, I started craving the post-walk clarity the way I used to crave the scroll. Clean, simple, mine.

Isolation stripped away the audience. There was no one to perform recovery for. That was its gift.

Private integrity became the only metric: what I did when every room was mine, every hour was open, and every excuse would be believed because no one was there to challenge it.

In 2022, life got loud again. Married Kelly. Three daughters joined our orbit with Emmy and Livvie. Our Tennessee house developed its own weather systems—dishwasher waterfalls, missing shoes treated like amber alerts, music from three rooms simultaneously. External structure returned dressed as family chaos. But the internal rails from lockdown held: phone still docks in the hallway, 90-second breathing still punctuates the day, Energy Ledger still prevents expensive mistakes.

Sometimes isolation reveals monsters. Sometimes it's just a mirror. For me, it was an X-ray showing fractures I'd been ignoring, plus a blueprint for reinforcement.

Your assignment (especially if days feel like one long hour):

Morning: List three energy deposits, three withdrawals. Keep it under sixty seconds. Sunlight counts. So does calling someone who loves you without needing anything.

2:25 PM: Stand up. Breathe for 90 seconds using the protocol. Walk for ten minutes. Drink water. Choose the next smallest honest action.

9 PM: Dock the phone in another room. Write NO NEW DECISIONS AFTER 9 on a card. Trust it more than your feelings.

Evening: Score your energy 1-10. Send a two-minute voice memo to someone with tomorrow's plan. Don't perform. Just report.

You don't need to be impressive. You need to be consistent. Energy first. Constraints second. Choices last.

Lockdown removed the scaffolding and revealed the skeleton. Alone together, I learned to be my own architecture. Integrity isn't a feeling—it's engineering. Boring, kind, and ready for the days when you're not.

Next, we'll take these healthy addictions and build environments that feed them automatically. We'll place friction where it saves you, remove it where it serves you, and let your spaces make the right thing effortless even when your willpower is gone.

CHAPTER 12

Becoming Addicted to the Right Things

My cravings didn't disappear—they migrated to places that loved me back.

They used to orbit the familiar darkness: the blue glow at 2 AM, the secret browser tab, the sugar hit that made my teeth ache but my nervous system briefly quiet. Then something shifted. The addiction machinery stayed intact, but I aimed it at different targets. Now the hit comes from the smell of the rubber floor in the gym and the desire for building muscle and lifting weight that comes from it, the way a barbell sits cold in my palms before the first rep, the specific exhaustion that tastes like copper pennies after a final rep. The way Kelly's hand finds my shoulder while I'm washing dishes and something deep in my spine remembers how to breathe. The chemistry didn't evaporate—I just taught it to hunt for things that pay compound interest instead of charging overdraft fees.

First, there's what I call my *Iron Addiction.*

March 2024, 5:10 AM. I stood in my underwear staring at the bathroom scale's verdict: 228 pounds. My reflection looked like someone had inflated a younger version of me—soft edges where there used to be definition, a belly that entered rooms slightly ahead of my chest. BMI: 30.1, technically obese, a word that tasted like failure marinated in shame. I could feel my shirt buttons working harder than they should. My knees complained on stairs. It was a far cry to my high weight of 267 in late 2019, but I wasn't going the direction I wanted after weighing in at 195 a year before.

I hired Marcus not because I was motivated but because I knew motivation was a liar. I needed someone who would show up at 6:00 AM on Mondays, Wednesdays, and Fridays with a clipboard and absolutely zero interest in my feelings. Someone who would say "three more" when my legs were screaming negotiations. Someone whose disappointment would cost more than the pain of showing up.

The first session, I threw up when I got to his home where he had converted his garage into his gym. Not dramatically—just quietly deposited my coffee and ego into the bushes while Marcus pretended to check his phone. "Happens to everyone," he lied kindly. My hands shook for an hour afterward. I couldn't hold my coffee mug steady. Everything tasted like pennies and regret.

But here's what happened: I came back.

We built it on a two-minute minimum because I'd learned that heroic goals are where consistency goes to die. The rule was simple: on the worst mornings, I just had to touch the barbell. That's it. Walk to the garage, put my hands on the cold metal, feel its weight. If that's all I had, the streak survived. But something about touching iron makes you want to lift it. Some mornings became one set of goblet squats. Some became a full session that left me baptized in sweat.

The fallback protocol saved me: if the barbell felt impossible, farmer's carry to the mailbox counted. Ten-minute incline walk if everything hurt. The point wasn't perfection—it was never letting the streak flatline. "Show up" was enough to keep the chain alive.

By September 2025, my body had reorganized itself: 204 pounds, BMI 25.4, muscle mass up 28%. But the mirror only tells part of the story. The training log tells the real one—pencil marks that track the small wars: "10 reps at 225, on bench press." "Added 10 pounds to farmer's carry, grip held." "PR on deadlift, 315x3, felt like flying."

The addiction transferred to micro-progressions. I started craving the moment at rep six when your muscles stage a protest vote and you override the democracy. The specific burn that spreads through your quads like warm honey. The way the seventh rep makes the eighth rep possible. The shower afterward became a victory ritual—steam mixing with sweat, forearms humming their own frequency, the particular exhaustion that feels like you've earned your place on earth.

The 5:10 AM alarm became Pavlovian. Shoes already positioned by the door like soldiers. Marcus would text "?" if I was two minutes late, just a question mark that carried the weight of accountability. After each session, I'd send Bobby a single line: "3x5 deadlifts, clean" or just a thumbs up. That tiny witness loop closed the circuit, made the session real, turned it from exercise into evidence.

Some days the numbers regressed—travel, sick kids, a night where sleep never arrived. The difference wasn't that I never failed; it was that I never let failure become identity. Miss Monday? Tuesday has a fallback waiting. The calendar's green chain became my new porn—I'd stare at those unbroken weeks of checkmarks with the same intensity I used to reserve for things that made me hate myself.

The Second Loop is the day when Food Became Fuel, Not Theatre.

For decades, eating was my emergency broadcast system. Chips at 10:30 PM weren't food—they were Xanax with crunch. The handful of candy at 2:45 PM was a peace treaty with an afternoon I didn't want to face. Opening the refrigerator at midnight, bathed in that clinical white light, wasn't hunger—it was hunting for a feeling that food could never actually provide.

The shift wasn't sudden or dramatic. It was systematic and boring, which is why it worked.

Sunday meal prep became meditation. The kitchen at 2 PM, music on, nobody home. Cutting board scarred from years of use. The rhythm of knife through chicken breast—precise, predictable, productive. Six pounds of protein portioned into glass containers that would stack in the fridge like ammunition for the week ahead. Vegetables chopped and waiting in clear containers at eye level—the path of least resistance redesigned.

We engineered the kitchen like a casino, but in reverse. Fruit bowl at eye level, not hidden in a drawer. Protein containers front and center, not buried behind condiments. Chips exiled to a high cabinet that requires a stepstool and makes a sound like judgment when it opens. The midnight refrigerator raid now met pre-cut carrots and hummus instead of leftover pizza. Friction where it saves you, ease where it serves you.

The food got simpler and my brain got sharper. Eggs at 7:10 AM, same pan, same two pieces of Ezekiel bread. Chicken and rice at noon with a fist of greens—not Instagram-worthy, just fuel that doesn't negotiate. Greek yogurt at 3 PM if training was heavy, with berries that burst like small celebrations. Dinner on an actual plate at an actual table, not standing at the counter or collapsed on the couch with a bag of something.

"Boring" started tasting like freedom. The 2:30 PM crash disappeared. My brain stayed bright after lunch instead of feeling like someone had thrown a blanket over my thoughts. Sleep turned clean and deep instead of that restless half-consciousness punctuated by refrigerator light. Kelly started saying "thanks for cooking" in a way that landed in my chest like a small warm stone.

The cravings didn't vanish—they relocated. I started missing the clarity when I ate garbage. Started craving the way my body hummed efficiently after simple fuel. The old hunt for sugar transformed into hunting for that bright-brain feeling after lunch, the clean energy that made the afternoon possible instead of something to survive.

Perhaps the biggest addiction, and by far the more fun one is *Scheduled Desire*

Kelly and I discussed whether we were becoming polite roommates who happened to share children and a mortgage. We'd kiss goodbye in the morning with the passion of coworkers clocking in. We'd fall asleep with our backs turned, two people protecting their own space in a bed meant for sharing. Sex had become a less than either of us wanted accident, something that happened when all the stars aligned and neither of us was too tired, too stressed, or too secretly resentful about the dishwasher.

So we did something that sounded ridiculous: we scheduled intimacy like a business meeting.

The 30-day challenge started as a joke with an edge of desperation. Five minutes minimum of sexual contact daily—touching, playing, connecting, whatever felt possible. We wrote it on the calendar in code: "P.M. Check-in." The kids thought it was budget meetings. It was, in a way—we were budgeting connection before bankruptcy arrived.

Night one felt like a middle school dance—awkward approach, nervous laughter, too much thinking. But we'd committed, so we followed through. Five minutes of kissing that reminded me why I fell in love with her mouth. Night two, she whispered "this is weird but good" while unbuttoning my shirt, and we both laughed until it wasn't weird anymore.

By week two, my body started expecting it. The "P.M. Check-in" became a warm thread running through the entire day. I'd catch her eye at breakfast and mouth "tonight," watch her smile spread slow like honey. The anticipation became foreplay that lasted hours. My hand would find her hip while we brushed teeth. She'd run her fingers across my shoulders while I cooked, just passing through but leaving electricity.

We missed three days in thirty—life happens, kids get sick, exhaustion wins. But twenty-seven out of thirty rewired something fundamental. The five-minute minimum removed performance pressure. Some nights were athletic and laughing. Some were exactly five minutes of being held like we both might break. Some turned into conversations with our bodies that we couldn't have with words.

The unexpected dividend: we became stronger allies. Disagreements that used to escalate into three-day cold wars now resolved in hours because our bodies remembered being on the same team twelve hours ago. I started listening to her with my whole face instead of waiting for my turn to be right. She started touching me casually again—hand on my back while reaching for coffee, fingers through my hair while we watched TV with the kids.

The oxytocin loop was real and measurable. Stress decreased like someone had finally found the volume knob. The house felt safer—not just for us but for our daughters, who could feel the difference in how we moved through rooms together. We picked better battles. We stopped weaponizing distance. We remembered why we chose this chaos together.

After the thirty days, we didn't maintain the daily streak. But now when we skip more than two days, my body notices the absence like missing a workout—something fundamental feels off. The craving moved from porn to person, from pixels to presence. I started wanting her the way I used to want escape—urgently, specifically, with my whole nervous system.

The Architecture of Good Addictions

Here's what lifting, meal prep, and scheduled sex taught me: addiction is just a learning loop your nervous system has memorized. The machinery doesn't care if the target is destructive or constructive—it just cares about reliable patterns. Cue → Behavior → Reward → Repeat until automatic.

The Iron Loop: 6:10 alarm → shoes by door → garage → barbell → effort → copper penny exhaustion → Marcus's nod → text to Bobby → green checkmark → identity deposit: "I'm someone who shows up."

The Fuel Loop: Sunday prep → containers at eye level → simple plate → bright brain afternoon → Kelly's "thanks for cooking" → clean sleep → easier tomorrow → crave the clarity.

The Connection Loop: Calendar reminder → eye contact at breakfast → anticipation all day → five-minute minimum → oxytocin flood → softer disagreements → unified parenting → desire for tomorrow's connection.

Each loop strengthened the others. Training made me want better fuel. Better fuel gave me energy for connection. Connection made me want to be someone worth desiring. The progression wasn't linear—it was a spiral moving upward, each revolution building on the last.

So, here's your assignment: Pick One and Start Small

Choose one keystone behavior. Not three. One.

Build the smallest possible version: two-minute workout, one meal prepped, three-minute intimacy.

Engineer the cues: shoes visible, protein at eye level, calendar reminder.

Design fallbacks: bodyweight squats count, protein shake counts, holding hands counts.

Mark the intrinsic reward: name the feeling you're hunting. "Clean exhaustion." "Bright brain." "Safe nervous system."

Get a witness: someone to text, someone to thank you, someone to notice.

Track the chain: visual proof that you're becoming someone who does this thing.

The transformation isn't in the numbers—228 to 204, 30 days of sex, 500 pounds moved. It's in the moment you realize you're craving the effort instead of the escape. When you miss the burn, the clarity, the connection. When your body starts pulling you toward things that pay you back instead of things that leave you empty.

My cravings didn't disappear. They just found better homes. Now they live in the garage where iron waits, in the kitchen where simple fuel builds tomorrow's energy, in the bedroom where connection replaces compulsion.

Next, we'll build environments that make these good addictions automatic—spaces designed to pull you toward health without requiring heroic willpower. Your rooms can be your rails. Let's build them.

CHAPTER 13

Truth Culture at Home

We found the truth behind the dryer, and it changed how we breathe.

The rattle had been there for months—a metallic complaint every time the dryer ran, like something trapped and trying to escape. One Saturday, I finally pulled the machine away from the wall. What spilled out was a small archaeological site of our avoidance: lint thick as winter insulation, two orphaned socks that belonged to no one, three quarters from 2019, a friendship bracelet with "BESTIE" barely visible through the dust, and a crumpled note in Livvie's bubble letters that just said "SORRY."

I stood there holding that note, feeling the weight of all our unspoken apologies trapped behind heavy things. The dryer had been choking on our secrets. When we cleared it—really cleared it, on our knees with the vacuum attachment—the machine exhaled. Clothes dried in half the time. The laundry room lost that burnt-dust smell I'd blamed on the house being old.

It was a three-dimensional metaphor delivered by Whirlpool: what you pretend isn't there still affects the atmosphere.

Our house was full of rattles. The way Kelly's jaw would tighten when I said "in a minute" for the third time. How Emmy would start sentences with "Never mind" when she saw my phone in my hand. The specific silence that fell after someone said "Fine" in that way that meant anything but. Five daughters, two adults, many pets, and one family—we were suffocating on swallowed words.

The Glass That Changed Everything

Tuesday, 5:47 PM. A crash from the kitchen, then silence—that particular silence that means someone's calculating whether to confess or flee. I walked in to find glass shards scattered like guilty stars across the tile, and three daughters suddenly fascinated by different corners of the ceiling.

My father would have lined us up. Would have made it about respect and responsibility and disappointment. I felt his script rising in my throat. Instead, I took a breath that went all the way to my feet and said:

"Truth beats trouble. Always. You have five minutes to tell me what happened. We'll clean it up together, no punishment for honesty. If I find out later from someone else, there will be consequences. Timer starts now."

Four minutes and thirty seconds later, Livvie appeared in the doorway, her whole body trying not to cry. "I was doing that TikTok dance—the one with the arm thing—and my elbow hit it and then I just... froze. I was going to clean it but I didn't know how to explain the missing glass and—"

"Thank you for telling me," I said, and watched her shoulders drop three inches. "I'm sorry I've made this kitchen feel like a place where hiding is safer than truth. Let's fix that. I'll get the broom. You bring the dustpan. We'll figure out the TikTok-safe zone after."

We swept in companionable silence. When we were done, I made hot chocolate—the real kind, with milk on the stove and the wooden spoon that's older than Emmy. Livvie sat at the counter watching the milk swirl.

"Dad?" she said. "That was different."

"Yeah," I said. "It was."

Making Truth Safe (Not Soft)

We started saying it at family meetings, at bedtime, in the car: *Telling the truth lowers the temperature in this house.* Not "honesty is the best policy"—that's a poster. This was a promise: your truth makes you safer here, not less safe.

The kids tested it like scientists:

Jenna, two days later: "I got a C on my history test." Waited for an explosion. Got: "Thanks for telling me. What do you need to understand it better?"

Emmy, that weekend: "I dented the car backing out." Braced for rage. Got: "I appreciate you telling me immediately. Let's look at it together and call insurance."

Livvie via text: 'I did not clean my room before I left for my mom's. I'm sorry. I'll make sure I work on that first when I come back."

Each truth told without punishment was a deposit in the trust account. Each calm response was proof that we meant it.

The Anatomy of Repair

We developed a formula, wrote it on an index card, taped it inside the pantry door where we could all see it:

The 24-Hour Repair Protocol:

1. Name what happened (no story, just facts).
2. Own your impact (how it landed on others).
3. Share what you'll do differently.
4. Ask what they need.
5. Set a check-back time.

Real repairs from our actual life:

Me to Kelly, after snapping about dishes: "I'm sorry I turned dishes into a prosecution. You were tired and I made it worse. My tone was sharp and dismissive—that probably felt like contempt. Next time I'll either do them myself quietly or ask once and let it go. I've set a reminder to handle dishes myself on your late-work nights. Can we take a walk and reset?"

Kelly to me, after a cold shoulder: "I'm sorry I went silent for two hours. I was hurt but I used distance as a weapon. That probably felt like abandonment. Next time I'll say 'I need twenty minutes to cool down' and then actually come back. Tonight I'm going to sit with you on the porch. What do you need from me?"

Me to Emmy, after missing her call: "I'm sorry I didn't pick up when you called from school. You needed me and I wasn't available. That probably felt like I only show up when it's convenient. I'm putting your number on special ring so it breaks through focus mode. Can you forgive me? What did you need to tell me?"

Emmy to Livvie, after a borrowed-shirt fight: "I'm sorry I wore your shirt without asking and then got mad when you called me out. That was entitled and mean. I'll wash it tonight and ask before borrowing. Also I'll let you borrow my green jacket this weekend. Are we good?"

These weren't performances. They were practice. Each repair made the next one easier, like we were building muscle memory for honesty.

The "Try Again" Revolution

The most powerful tool we installed was stupidly simple: the do-over.

Scene: Wednesday dinner. Livvie asks for help with homework. I'm three emails deep in my head and say, "Can't you figure it out yourself? You're in high school."

Her face shifts—that micro-expression teenagers perfect where hurt hides behind indifference.

Kelly touches my hand. "Want to try that again?"

I stop. Breathe. Reset my face. "I'm sorry, Livvie. Let me try again: I'm in the middle of something stressful, but your homework matters. Can we look at it together at 7:30? I'll give you my full attention then."

Livvie's face softens. "Yeah, 7:30 works."

Five words—"Want to try that again?"—became our family's ctrl+z. We use it everywhere:

Kid to parent: "This dinner is gross."
"Try again?"
"I'm not hungry for this. Can I make a sandwich?"
"Yes."

Partner to partner: "You always—"
"Try again without always?"
"Tonight when you did X, I felt Y."
"Thank you. Let me respond to that."

Parent to teen: "Your room is disgusting."

"Let me try again: Your room needs attention. Pick two things to handle tonight."

"I can do laundry and trash."

"Perfect."

The genius is that it stops the spiral before damage happens. It's not about perfection—it's about practice. Every do-over builds the neural pathway for saying it better the first time.

The YouTube & Instagram Incident

I noticed Livvie had been loading YouTube and uploading videos—and using Instagram to view similar content—that we had never agreed were appropriate.

The old me would have reacted fast and loud. Confiscation. Lectures. A sharp line drawn in anger.

Instead, I waited for a quiet moment and sat down with her.

"Hey," I said, "I came across some videos you were loading and uploading on YouTube, and some content on Instagram, that we hadn't agreed on. I'm not here to blow this up. I want to understand what was going on."

She hesitated, bracing for impact. When it didn't come, she talked. About trends. About wanting to participate. About not thinking through where the line actually was—or what to do when curiosity got ahead of judgment.

"I appreciate you being honest," I said. "Here's the reality: those videos need to come down. That part isn't optional."

She nodded. No arguing. No deflection. She removed the videos herself.

"And here's the rest," I continued. "We already have accountability in place for YouTube and Instagram, and that still stands. We're not throwing it out—we're recommitting to it. But we're also adding clarity: if this happens again, it may mean losing access to one or both platforms. Not as punishment, but as a consequence."

She agreed. Fully. Owned it.

What mattered most wasn't that the videos were removed—it was that accountability wasn't something done *to* her. It was something she chose to step back into.

The Reckoning

Six months into our truth culture experiment, something shifted. The house felt different—like someone had opened windows we didn't know were painted shut.

Conversations stopped having that underwater quality where everyone's holding their breath. Apologies became specific and boring instead of dramatic productions. "Sorry" turned into "Sorry for X, impact was Y, next time Z."

The daughters started telling us things before they became secrets:

- "This boy is texting me and it's getting uncomfortable."
- "I think I failed my math test."
- "Sarah's party has older kids and I'm nervous."
- "I don't think I like soccer anymore."

They weren't confessing. They were consulting. Truth had become safer than silence.

When Kelly and I Hit the Wall

Tuesday night, 11 PM. We're in bed, both scrolling, both pretending the other doesn't exist. The distance between us might as well be an ocean.

"I don't like us right now," Kelly says to the ceiling.

"Me neither," I say.

"Want to try again?" she asks.

"From where?"

"From Tuesday morning when you said you'd handle camp forms and didn't."

"Okay. I'm sorry I dropped the camp forms. I wrote it down but didn't set a reminder. You had to scramble and probably felt like I don't see your labor. Next time I'll either do it immediately or calendar it with an alert. I'll handle them tonight before I sleep."

She turns toward me. "I'm sorry I've been cold for three days instead of just telling you I was pissed. That probably felt like punishment. Next time I'll say 'I'm angry about X' within the hour."

We're facing each other now. The phones are down. The ocean becomes a river, then a stream, then just the space between two bodies that remember how to meet.

Your Assignment: Build Your Truth Culture

Week 1: Make truth safe

- Say out loud: "Truth beats trouble in this house".
- When someone tells a hard truth, respond with "Thank you for telling me" before anything else.
- Count to five before responding to any confession.

Week 2: Install the 24-hour rule

- Write the repair protocol somewhere visible.
- Practice one repair daily (even tiny ones).
- When you miss the 24-hour window, repair the miss.

Week 3: Launch "Try again"

- Introduce it gently: "Want to try saying that differently?"
- Use it on yourself first: "Let me try that again".
- Celebrate successful do-overs immediately.

Week 4: Start the Sunday Summit

- 15 minutes, no more.
- One truth, one repair, one gratitude per person.
- No fixing, just witnessing.

The lint will keep accumulating behind the dryer. That's what lint does in houses where humans live and clothes get worn and life happens fast. But now we know: you can move the heavy thing, clear the space, and breathe better. You can make truth safer than secrets. You can repair faster than resentment builds.

The house still gets messy. We still snap, slam, and say things sideways. But now we have a way back to each other that doesn't require perfection—just the next honest sentence, the next specific repair, the next try-again.

Next, we'll take this truth culture and build systems for sharing power—chores that assign themselves, boundaries that everyone helps design, and family agreements that make democracy possible without chaos. But first, we breathe the cleaner air.

PART IV

Growth: High Performance, Critical Thinking, and Purpose

Think Clean to Live Clean: Critical Thinking as a Sobriety Tool

By 2:30 PM, I can tell if I'm going to relapse tonight. Not by my willpower—by the quality of my questions.

Bad days sound like this in my head: *What's the fastest way to stop feeling this? Why does everyone else have it easier? When will this craving end?* These questions are already drunk. They stumble toward the nearest exit.

Clean days ask different questions: *What's the next smallest action that serves my purpose? What need is this urge trying to meet? What would future-me thank present-me for?* These questions are sober. They build bridges instead of burning them.

The difference between sobriety and relapse often comes down to thirty seconds of thinking. Not heroic thinking—structured thinking. A framework I can run even when my brain feels like it's on fire.

The Night I Interviewed My Own Urge

11:47 PM, Tuesday. Kelly's asleep beside me, her breathing deep and trusting. The phone sits on my nightstand like a loaded gun with a warm grip. The familiar whisper starts: *Just check the news. Five minutes. You've been good all week.*

My thumb hovers over the screen. The old me would already be three apps deep, chasing dopamine down rabbit holes that all lead to the same shameful dawn. But there's a coffee-stained 3x5 card propped against the lamp—my field sobriety test for thoughts. I grab it like a life raft.

Purpose: Protect sleep, tomorrow's workout, and my integrity with Kelly.

Question: What's the smallest action that honors rest right now?

Information: I slept 5.5 hours last night. Alarm set for 6:10 AM. Phone dock is 23 steps down the hall (I counted). Browser blocker activates at midnight. Last time I docked early, I fell asleep in six minutes. Last time I "quickly checked," 47 minutes vanished.

Assumptions: "I need novelty to unwind." Test: Is this true? Can I get novelty from the Jack Reacher paperback on my nightstand?

Inferences: If I pick up the phone, statistics say I'll scroll for 40+ minutes, sleep debt will compound, tomorrow's workout will suffer.

Implications: Tired me is impatient me. Impatient me snaps at kids. Snapping creates repair debt. Repair debt creates distance. Distance creates conditions for relapse.

Point of View: Future-me at 6:10 AM would beg current-me to put the phone down. Kelly trusts me to protect our boundaries. The app developers profit from my insomnia.

Standards Check:

- Clarity: The choice is binary—dock or scroll.
- Accuracy: The data about scroll time is from my own screen reports.
- Relevance: Every fact connects to tomorrow's success.
- Logic: Scrolling directly contradicts my stated purpose.
- Fairness: I deserve rest, not empty stimulation.
- Significance: This moment determines tomorrow's trajectory.

Action: I do 90 seconds of 4-2-8-2 breathing. My heart rate drops from race to walk. I stand up (harder than it should be), walk the 23 steps, dock the phone with a decisive click. Back in bed, I read exactly one chapter about Reacher solving problems with clarity instead of his fists. Lights out by 12:03. Asleep by 12:09.

The urge didn't disappear. I just out-thought it.

The Framework That Saves My Ass Daily

I didn't invent this. I stole it from Linda Elder and Richard Paul's critical thinking model and turned it into a pocket-sized sobriety tool. Seven elements, eight standards, one minute to run:

The Elements (what to examine):

- Purpose: Why am I thinking/acting?
- Question: What exactly am I trying to answer?
- Information: What facts do I have? What's missing?
- Assumptions: What am I taking for granted?
- Inferences: What conclusions am I drawing?
- Implications: If I act on this conclusion, what follows?
- Point of View: What would others see? What would future-me see?

The Standards (how to judge quality):

- Clarity: Can I state this simply?
- Accuracy: Is this actually true?
- Relevance: Does this matter to my purpose?
- Depth: Am I at the root or trimming leaves?
- Breadth: What else could be true?
- Logic: Do the pieces fit together?
- Fairness: Am I stacking the deck?
- Significance: Am I focusing on what counts?

This isn't philosophy—it's prevention. Every urge, conflict, and decision gets better when I run it through this grid.

Steelmanning the Enemy

2:27 PM, Wednesday. The afternoon urge arrives like a punctual demon. My brain starts chanting: *Chips. Phone. Couch. Chips. Phone. Couch.*

The old me would white-knuckle through it or shame myself: *You're weak. You're pathetic. You're going to fail.* That's like fighting fire with gasoline.

Now I steelman the urge—I articulate its best possible argument:

"I want chips and scrolling because I've been focused for three hours straight. My brain is legitimately depleted. I need novelty to reset my attention, salt to wake up my mouth, and movement to discharge the sitting energy. This isn't weakness—it's biology requesting resources."

Holy shit. When I respect the urge, it stops screaming.

"Okay," I tell it. "You're right. We need novelty, fuel, and movement. Here's what we'll do: Walk to the corner playing that new album you downloaded. Drink the full water bottle. Eat the apple slices and almonds I pre-cut for exactly this moment. Then we'll do five minutes of that YouTube drum solo compilation you love."

The urge considers this. It's getting its needs met, just through different channels.

I run the card:

- Purpose: Restore energy for the next work block.
- Question: What refreshes without stealing tomorrow?
- Information: Walks restore focus (proven); scrolling fragments it (also proven).
- Assumptions: "I deserve instant relief" → Relief can take ten minutes and last longer.
- Implications: Walk = energy; scroll = energy debt.
- POV: 4:30 PM me needs 2:30 PM me to choose wisely.
- Standards: All green lights toward the walk.

I walk. The November air hits my face like a gentle slap from someone who loves me. My legs remember they exist. The new album is better than scrolling—it's curated novelty instead of random noise. I return after twelve minutes with actual energy instead of the fake fizz that scrolling provides.

The urge got respected, redirected, and satisfied. We both won.

Conflict Resolution in Real Time

Thursday evening. Kelly says, "I feel alone at bedtime."

My immediate internal response: *But I did dishes! I handled kid pickup! I fixed the sink!* This is the prosecutor mind, building a case for my innocence.

Stop. Run the card:

Purpose: Understand and repair, not win,
Question: What is she actually asking for?
Information: She said "alone at bedtime," not "you don't do enough".
Assumptions: I'm assuming this is about chore equity. What if it's about emotional presence?
Inferences: If I list my contributions, I'm answering a question she didn't ask.
Implications: Defending proves her point—I'm not hearing her.
POV: From her position, I might physically be home but emotionally AWOL.
Standards: Fairness says her feeling is valid regardless of my chore count.

"You feel alone when we're supposed to be together," I say instead. "That must be really lonely. What would help you feel more connected at bedtime?"

Her shoulders drop. "Just... be there. Not on your phone. Not planning tomorrow. Just there with me for ten minutes."

"I can do that. Starting tonight. I'll set a reminder for 9:20 to wrap up whatever I'm doing."

We solved in two minutes what could have become a three-day cold war. The card turned me from prosecutor to partner.

Building Plans That Actually Happen

I used to make plans for a person who didn't exist—Future Me who had infinite energy, zero interruptions, and monk-like discipline. That person never showed up, so neither did the results.

Now I plan for the actual human who will execute—tired, distracted, tempted, real.

Friday morning, planning the week:

Purpose: Complete Project X draft by Friday without sacrificing family or fitness.

Question: What's the minimum viable outline and when are my real windows?

Information:

- Two confirmed 90-minute blocks (Tuesday/Thursday mornings).
- Kids' recital Thursday evening (non-negotiable).
- Energy peaks at 8-10 AM, crashes at 2-3 PM.
- Last three "I'll write at night" attempts: 0% success rate.

Assumptions: "I write best under pressure" - Translation: I avoid starting to protect my ego from judgment.

Implications: If I wait until Thursday, I risk spillover into family time and stress that affects everyone.

POV: Friday Me wants Monday Me to start immediately. My family wants me present Thursday night. My editor wants clarity over perfection.

Standards Check:

- Significance: Outline matters more than font choice.
- Logic: Front-load the hard thinking when energy is high.
- Accuracy: My "night writing" fantasy has zero supporting evidence.

Action:

- Block Tuesday 8-10 AM now (calendar, door sign, phone docked).
- Create outline in 25 minutes TODAY.
- Thursday 8-10 AM for draft.
- Email editor: "Draft Friday noon, feedback welcome on structure".

The plan respects reality instead of requiring heroics.

The Daily Card Habit

I carry blank 3x5 cards like a smoker carries cigarettes—always within reach, used at the first sign of craving. They live in my gym bag, truck console, kitchen drawer, nightstand. The format is always the same, muscle memory now:

Morning workout resistance:

- Purpose: Strength for life.
- Question: What's the minimum that keeps the streak?
- Information: Slept 6 hours, legs sore, Marcus expects me.
- Assumption: "I need to feel good to train" → False, I need to train to feel good.
- Implication: Skip = shame spiral risk.
- POV: Noon Me will be proud or pissed.
- Action: Show up, half weight if needed.

Tense text from ex:

- Purpose: Protect kids' stability.
- Question: What response serves co-parenting?
- Information: She's stressed about holidays, history of escalation.
- Assumption: This is an attack → Maybe it's anxiety.
- Implication: Fight = kids feel it.
- POV: Kids need boring parents.
- Action: "Let's talk Sunday 2 PM when we're both fresh".

Amazon cart at midnight:

- Purpose: Use money wisely.
- Question: Need or want?
- Information: Bank balance, actual holes in life.
- Assumption: Buying brings relief → Temporary at best.
- Implication: Tomorrow's guilt, partner's questions.
- POV: Morning Me says close the laptop.
- Action: Screenshot cart, revisit Sunday if still relevant.
- Each card takes 45-90 seconds. The ROI is thousands of better decisions.

Clean Thinking With Others

This isn't just internal. I've started infecting others with the framework:

Team meeting: "Before we dive in—what's our purpose for these 30 minutes? What question are we actually trying to answer?"

With kids: "Help me understand your point of view on this rule. What feels unfair about it?"

With Kelly: "I realize I was assuming you could read my mind about dinner plans. That was unfair. What information did you need that I didn't provide?"

With Bobby: "My inference is that I'm bothering you with these calls. Accuracy check?"

The framework becomes a shared language for cleaner conversations. We fight less about positions and more about purposes. We check assumptions before they become arguments.

The Compound Effect

Six months of daily cards has changed my mental weather:

- Urges feel less like commands, more like requests I can negotiate.
- Conflicts resolve faster because I identify the real question sooner.
- Plans actually happen because they're built for real me, not fantasy me.
- Sleep comes easier because I've interviewed and dismissed the day's anxieties.
- My sobriety feels less like willpower and more like clarity.

The biggest shift: I've stopped treating my thoughts like truth and started treating them like drafts. Every thought gets a quick edit before I let it drive behavior.

Your Assignment: Start With One Card

Today, right now, grab any piece of paper. Write these prompts:

- Purpose:
- Question:
- Information:
- Assumptions (test one):
- Inferences:
- Implications:
- POV (other/future):

Use it once before noon on any decision. Use it once tonight on any urge.

Tomorrow, make three cards. Put them where problems live—nightstand for nighttime urges, dashboard for traffic rage, desk drawer for work anxiety.

This week, steelman one urge. Give it full respect: "You're trying to meet the need for X." Then redirect: "Here's a cleaner way to get X."

Think clean to live clean. Sloppy thoughts create sloppy days. Clear thoughts create clear paths. The framework isn't magical—it's just more reliable than hoping your tired, triggered, tempted brain will somehow make good choices without structure.

Next, we'll scale this clarity to entire environments—how to design your spaces and systems so the right choice becomes the easy choice, even when your thinking is compromised. But first, master the card. One clean thought at a time.

High Performance Habits for Recovery and Beyond (Or: Why I Stopped Waiting to Be Fixed Before Building Something)

"I'm scared I'll outrun my recovery if I go bigger."

The words fell out of my mouth into a Monday morning coaching circle, landing like glass on concrete. Twenty recovering addicts stared at me. My palms were soaking through my jeans. The edge of my planner was cutting into my thumb because I was gripping it like it might run away.

This wasn't NA. This was a high-performance coaching group. But half the room was in recovery, and we all had the same look—like kids who'd been caught planning something dangerous.

Then the room exhaled with me. Because finally—finally—someone said what we were all thinking: What if getting better means we have to stay small forever?

The Waiting Room Trap

For eighteen months, I sat in NA meetings believing I had to earn my way back to life. Step 4, Step 8, Step 9—make amends, clear wreckage, then maybe, someday, if you're very good and very sorry, you can think about building something.

The message was everywhere: You broke things, so you don't get to create things. Not yet. Maybe not ever. Just be grateful you're not dead.

Don't misunderstand—NA saved my life. Those rooms gave me language for my pain, witnesses to my walking disaster, and a framework for facing what I'd done. I still go to meetings. Every Monday, 6 AM, same shitty coffee, same beautiful broken people. The program is medicine, and I'll take it for life.

But somewhere between "Keep coming back" and "Easy does it," I absorbed poison: the idea that healing and growth are sequential. That you have to be completely fixed before you're allowed to build. That ambition in early recovery is just another form of addiction.

Then Tuesday happened.

The Tuesday That Cracked Me Open

October 2024, 2 PM, hiding in my home office, scrolling through Brendon Burchard's book on my phone while pretending to work. I'd bought it six months earlier in a moment of 3 AM hope, then hid it like porn because "high performance" felt like contraband for someone only two years clean.

I'm reading about his "Clarity" practice when my sponsor texts: "You missed noon meeting. You good?"

I stare at the text. Then at the book. Then at my calendar where I'd scheduled "Deep Work" over meeting time.

I text back: "I'm good. Working on something."

"Working or avoiding?"

Fuck. He always knows.

"Both," I type. Then add: "Reading about high performance. Feel like a fraud."

Phone rings immediately.

"You know what's fraudulent?" he says without a hello. "Pretending you're not ambitious. You were ambitious as an addict—you just aimed it at destroying yourself. Now aim it at building. Same energy, different target."

"But what if I relapse because I take on too much?"

"What if you relapse because you take on too little? Boredom killed more addicts than busy ever did."

He hangs up. No goodbye. Classic sponsor move.

I sit there, book in one hand, phone in the other, feeling something crack open in my chest. Not breaking. Opening.

The Revolutionary Idea Hidden in Plain Sight

Here's what Brendon's work taught me that no recovery room ever did: Growth doesn't wait for healing to be complete. Growth IS healing in motion.

But let me be clear—I didn't read his book and transform overnight. I read it and fought it. Tried his practices and failed spectacularly. Cried over my planner at 5 AM because writing "I am a recovering father" made me remember every school play I missed high.

Kelly found me one morning, snot on my face, planner soaked with tears.

"Maybe do this after coffee," she said.

"It's supposed to be before coffee. First thing. Clear mind."

"Your mind is never clear at 5 AM. Your mind at 5 AM is a conspiracy theorist with a grudge."

We both laughed. She was right. Growth is messy as fuck, especially when you're growing in the wreckage you created.

Why High Performance Habits Are Recovery Medicine

Here's the thing nobody tells you: Brendon's framework—Clarity, Energy, Courage, Productivity, Influence—isn't about grinding harder. It's about growing smarter while your bones are still mending.

But I learned this the hard way. Tried to do all five habits perfectly my first week. By Thursday, I was so overwhelmed I almost convinced myself that buying whiskey was "research for understanding my triggers." That's addict logic—take something helpful and weaponize it against yourself.

My sponsor laughed when I told him. "You tried to get a PhD in recovery in a week. How very alcoholic of you."

So I started smaller. One habit. One week. One mess at a time.

Clarity: The Sentence That Saved My Sanity (Eventually)

In NA, they tell you "Just for today." Beautiful. Essential. But for my brain, incomplete. My brain needs more words to argue with.

Brendon teaches you to write a clarity sentence every morning: "I am X who does Y so I can Z."

My first attempt: "I am a piece of shit who's trying not to be a piece of shit so my family doesn't leave."

Kelly read it over my shoulder. "Maybe something more... aspirational?"

Second attempt: "I am a recovering father who keeps promises."

"Better. Still sounds like a hostage video."

Two weeks of terrible sentences before I landed on something real:

"Just for today, I am a recovering father-athlete who builds while healing, so I will protect three hours of deep work AND make it to dinner because my sobriety serves my family and my work serves my purpose."

See what happened? Recovery isn't separate from performance—it's the foundation that makes performance possible. But it took me seventeen drafts and two anxiety attacks to figure that out.

Energy: Recovery Rooms + Iron + Whatever the Fuck Works

Tuesday, 6 AM: NA meeting. "My name is Brian, and I'm an addict."

Tuesday, 7:30 AM: Gym with my trainer. "Three more reps. Don't you dare quit."

Tuesday, 8:45 AM: Parking lot, crying because both were hard and I'm tired of everything being hard.

Same morning. Same mess of a human. Different medicines for different wounds.

The meeting reminds me I'm not unique in my disaster. The gym proves I can do hard things without dying. The crying proves I'm still human. All three are true. All three are happening NOW, not someday when I'm "ready."

But here's what actually works—what Brendon calls "Release Tension, Set Intention" but what I call "Dump the Shit, Aim the Energy":

After the meeting, before the gym, I sit in my car for two minutes. I write one thing I'm releasing (today: the fantasy that I'll ever be a moderate drinker) and one thing I'm bringing (today: proof that I can lift heavy things without dropping them).

It's not profound. It's not pretty. But it bridges the gap between "I'm an addict" and "I'm an athlete." Both true. Both me. Both happening right fucking now.

Courage: Making Amends While Making Waves (The Wednesday Disaster)

Wednesday, October 2024. Two courage assignments on my calendar:

10 AM: Call my brother about the $3,000 I stole in 2019.
2 PM: Pitch a $15K workshop to a client.

Old recovery logic says: Complete all amends first, THEN pursue opportunities. But that's like saying heal completely before you try walking. You'll die in bed, fully apologetic but completely useless.

10 AM call to my brother:
"Hey. I need to acknowledge the three grand I took. I was sick, but that's not an excuse. I have $500 now, can do $500 a month for five months. I'm sorry for the betrayal. What else do you need from me?"

Silence. Then: "You sound different."

"I'm sober. And working."

"Both?"

"Both."

"Bobby said you were trying to do too much."

"Bobby thinks making my bed is too much."

He laughs. "Fair. Send the $500. We're good."

I hang up shaking. Amends are supposed to feel cleansing. This feels like I swallowed glass.

2 PM client pitch:
My voice cracks twice. I'm sweating through my shirt. But I present the workshop outline like my life depends on it, because in a way, it does. I need to build more than I destroyed. The math has to work out eventually.

"This is exactly what we need," the client says. "When can you start?"

I almost say "when I'm ready." Instead, I say "Monday."

Both calls happened with the same shaky voice. Both were necessary. Both were terrifying. Both were possible because I stopped waiting to be worthy.

Productivity: Building While Broken (The Thursday Reality)

Thursday, 10:30 AM. PQO block—Prolific Quality Output. Brendon's fancy term for "shut up and create something."

I'm writing curriculum for recovering executives. My target audience? People exactly like me—high achievers whose ambition almost killed them, who've been told to "keep it simple" when their souls are screaming for complexity.

10:31 AM: Blank page paralysis.

10:35 AM: Check email instead.

10:37 AM: Remember I'm supposed to be in recovery from avoiding hard things.

10:38 AM: Type one sentence: "You're allowed to want more than sobriety."

10:39 AM: Delete it. Too preachy.

10:40 AM: Type: "I spent eighteen months in recovery rooms afraid to admit I wanted to build something bigger than my amends list."

Better. True-er. Still scared someone from NA will read it and revoke my clean time.

11:47 AM: 1,200 words done. Messy, raw, probably too honest. But done.

12:52 PM: Draft sent to editor.

1:00 PM: Text to sponsor: "Productive morning. Staying clean. Sorry about missing noon meeting."

"You make meetings or you make excuses. Which one you want to make tomorrow?"

"Meeting."

"Good. Bring coffee. The good kind. Your amends to the group for today."

The work and the recovery aren't separate. They're the same project: becoming useful while admitting I'm still broken.

Influence: Leading From the Middle of the Mess

Friday evening. I'm speaking at an NA meeting. The topic they gave me: "Keeping It Simple."

I almost laugh. Instead, I say:

"They tell you to keep it simple. And early on, that's life-saving advice. When I was three days clean, 'don't use' was all the complexity I could handle. But some of us are built for complexity. Some of us heal BY building. Some of us need to create as much as we need to recover. And that's not ego—that's design."

A young woman raises her hand. "But what if I relapse because I took on too much?"

"What if you relapse because you took on too little?" I respond. "I know that's not what you're supposed to say in these rooms. But boredom almost killed me in month six. Under-achievement felt like drowning in slow motion. What if the safest thing you can do is build a life so engaging you don't want to escape it?"

Old-timer in the back: "That sounds like ego."

"Maybe. Or maybe it sounds like someone who knows that 'just don't use' isn't enough for everyone. Maybe some of us need 'don't use AND build something meaningful.' Both. Same day. Same person."

After the meeting, three people ask me about high performance in recovery. The old-timer corners me by the coffee: "You're playing with fire, kid."

"I'm playing with my actual life. The fire was killing myself slowly with substances. This is called living."

He walks away shaking his head. But the three people who approached me? They're still texting me. Still building. Still sober.

The Integration: Recovery Rooms AND Boardrooms (The Actual Messy Week)

Here's my actual week, not the Instagram version:

Monday: 6 AM NA meeting where I share about money fear. 9 AM team meeting where I project confidence about Q4. Both are true. Both are me. The cognitive dissonance gives me a headache by noon.

Tuesday: Sponsor call about Step 4 resentments—specifically, resenting people who can drink normally. Client call about Q4 objectives—specifically, a company happy hour I need to navigate. I take Advil after both calls.

Wednesday: Therapy for trauma at 10 AM—ugly cry about my dad. Training session at 5 PM—PR my deadlift. Text my therapist: "I lifted 315 pounds four hours after sobbing about abandonment. Is that progress or avoidance?" She texts back: "Yes."

Thursday: Read recovery literature (boring as fuck but necessary). Read business strategy (also boring but differently necessary). Write content that bridges both. Half my recovery friends think I'm too ambitious. Half my business friends think I'm too damaged. Both are probably right.

Friday: Make an amends call—goes terribly, she hangs up on me. Make a sales call—goes perfectly, $8K contract. Make dinner for my family—burn the chicken, everyone eats it anyway. All three are what happened. All three are my actual life.

The Permission Slip You've Been Waiting For (With Conditions)

Let me be crystal fucking clear: If you're in your first 30 days, ignore everything about high performance. Don't use. Go to meetings. Call your sponsor. Eat food. Sleep. Repeat. The fancy shit can wait.

But if you're stable in your recovery—let's say 90 days without using—and you're sitting in rooms feeling like you have to apologize for wanting more, like ambition is a character defect, like you have to choose between recovery and achievement, let me tell you what I wish someone had told me:

You're allowed to do both. Messily. Imperfectly. Starting now.

You're allowed to grow while you heal—just don't pretend the growth will be pretty.

You're allowed to build while you mend—just know you'll cry at inappropriate times.

You're allowed to lead while you learn—just admit when you don't know shit.

You're allowed to serve while you recover—just don't use service to avoid your steps.

You're allowed to achieve while you make amends—just remember achievement doesn't erase what you did.

The Weekly Practice That Actually Works (After You Fail Six Times)

Every Sunday, I do Brendon's planning. But it took me two months to figure out how to make it work with recovery. Here's what actually sticks:

CLARITY - The Both/And Sentence:

"I am a recovering _________ who _________, so this week I will _________ AND _________ because _________."

This week's actual sentence: "I am a recovering father who sometimes wants to run away, so this week I will complete three deep work blocks AND attend four meetings because my family needs me present and I need to build something that matters more than vodka."

Not pretty. But true.

ENERGY - The Non-Negotiables:

Recovery thing: Monday, Wednesday, Friday meetings (no excuses, no client calls during).

Growth thing: Tuesday, Thursday deep work blocks (no meetings during, no recovery guilt).

Integration: Saturday morning—write about both for 30 minutes, try to make sense of the week.

COURAGE - The Dual Assignment:

One amends/repair: Text my daughter's teacher about missing the conference while drunk last year.

One growth risk: Raise my coaching prices by 30% (I'm worth more than I charge).

PRODUCTIVITY - The Building Blocks:

What will you create that serves others in recovery? One blog post about being ambitious in recovery.

What will you build that proves recovery works? A business that generates more than I ever stole.

INFLUENCE - The Truth Telling:

Who needs to see that both are possible? The three guys from meeting who text me about feeling stuck.

What story will you tell? This one. The messy one. The true one.

The Truth That Nobody Wants to Admit

You know what's more dangerous than growing while recovering? Not growing while recovering.

I've watched more people relapse from boredom than from busy. I've seen more go back out because life felt empty than full. Stagnation is a relapse fuel. Under-achievement breeds resentment. Playing small doesn't keep you safe—it keeps you sick.

The rooms of recovery gave me my life back. But learning to build while healing—that's what made life worth keeping.

Not someday. Not after all 12 steps. Not when I'm "ready." Now. Today. While I'm still messy. While my hands still shake during amends. While I still cry in therapy. While I still check my sober date app every morning to make sure the days are still adding up.

Your Assignment (Start Messy, Stay Consistent):

1. Write your both/and sentence. Make it true, not pretty: "I am recovering AND _________. This week I will heal by _________ AND grow by _________."
2. Schedule both in your actual calendar. Meeting at 6 AM. Deep work at 9 AM. Both real. Both protected.
3. Find one thing that serves both. For me, it's writing. For you, it might be different. But find the overlap.

4. Tell someone in recovery about your ambitions. Watch them either light up or freak out. Both responses are data.
5. Tell someone in your professional life you're in recovery. Not the whole story. Just "I'm in recovery and it makes me better at my job." Watch their face reorganize.

The Final Truth

Monday morning, coaching circle, after I admitted my fear about outrunning my recovery, my mentor said something that rewired my brain:

"What if you can't outrun your recovery? What if recovery IS the vehicle, not the thing you're running from? What if every ambitious thing you build is just recovery in a different costume?"

I'm crying as I write this. Because he's right. Because I spent so long believing I had to choose. Because I wasted so many months in waiting rooms when I could have been building.

Recovery without growth is survival—necessary but not sufficient.

Growth without recovery is dangerous—I've got the wreckage to prove it.

Recovery WITH growth? That's life. Messy, complicated, sometimes contradictory life.

You didn't get clean to be safe and small. You got clean to be useful and real. And real means all of you—the parts that go to meetings AND the parts that want to build an empire, the person making amends AND making waves, the addict AND the achiever.

Both. At the same time. Starting now. Starting messy. Starting before you're ready.

The rooms will keep you clean. High performance will help you build something worth staying clean for. You need both. You deserve both. You can have both.

Even if it makes you cry at your desk on a Thursday at 10:47 AM while writing curriculum for recovering executives.

Even if the old-timers shake their heads.

Even if you have to figure it out one failed week at a time.

Stop waiting for permission. Stop waiting to be fixed. Start building the life that makes relapse look boring by comparison.

Both. And. Now.

CHAPTER 16

From Recovery to Purpose (Or: How Helping Other People Saves Your Ass)

The first year of sobriety, I counted days. The second year, I started counting people.

Day 1: Survived.
Day 30: Still here.
Day 365: Holy shit, I made it.
Day 400: Wait... now what?

That's when the real terror hit: I'm sober—but what the fuck am I sober FOR?

The Knock at the Grocery Store

Tuesday, 7 PM, frozen food aisle. I'm staring at pizza options like they contain the secret to happiness when I hear: "Brian? From the courthouse?"

I turn. It's a dad I'd seen in family court three months ago—the one whose hands shook so hard the papers rattled like leaves. Now he's holding a basket with those sad single-guy microwave dinners and wearing the specific exhaustion that comes from surviving another custody exchange without drinking.

"How did you..." he starts, then stops. His eyes are doing that thing where they're trying not to water. "How did you not lose your mind?"

I almost laugh. Almost tell him about October 2023 when I sat in my car outside the courthouse for forty minutes because I couldn't stop shaking. Almost mention the bathroom stall where I did breathing exercises while other dads threw up from anxiety.

Instead, I say, "I did lose it. Multiple times. I just built systems to find it again faster."

We end up talking for twelve minutes between the frozen peas and ice cream. His Friday nights are killing him—kids go to mom's at 5 PM, house goes quiet, brain goes dark. I know that specific silence. It sounds like failure and vodka.

I grab a receipt from my pocket, flip it over, and write:

5:15 - Walk out door (can't spiral while moving)
5:30 - Call someone (voice breaks the loop)
7:00 - Gym class (exhausted body = quiet mind)

He takes the receipt like I just handed him a winning lottery ticket.

"This Friday?" he asks.

"Every Friday. Text me Saturday morning. One word: 'survived' or 'struggled.' We'll adjust from there."

That Saturday, 7:43 AM, my phone buzzes: "Survived. Thank you."

That's when I learned: My mess had become my message. But more importantly—my message had become my medicine.

Service as Selfish Strategy

Here's what nobody tells you about helping others in recovery: It's not noble. It's selfish. And that's why it works.

When I help another divorced dad plan his Friday night, I'm not being generous. I'm being strategic. Because if I tell him to dock his phone at 9 PM, I can't be scrolling at 9:15. If I tell him to hit the gym instead of the bar, I better have my gym bag ready. If I tell him the spiral always starts with "just one," I can't pretend my "just one look" at Instagram is different.

Hypocrisy feels too much like relapse. And I'm allergic to both.

Every person I help is another rope tying me to shore. Not because I'm their savior—I can barely save myself most days. But because when someone's counting on your Thursday wisdom for their Friday survival, you can't throw away your Wednesday. That's not pressure. That's architecture.

The Service Sprint (Small Moves, Real Impact)

I don't run a nonprofit.
I don't make content for attention.
I'm not here to inspire you.

What I do is smaller. And it actually works.

Every Thursday, I give one person one hour to build momentum where their loop keeps breaking it.

That's it.

Not therapy.
Not coaching you through your childhood.
Not "let's talk about how you feel."

One hour to identify the pressure point, strip out unnecessary decisions, and install a system that survives real life.

Because the problem isn't that you don't want better.
The problem is that when the load hits, your loop takes over and choice disappears.

Last week, it was someone whose nights kept undoing their mornings.
The week before, someone who looked fine on the outside and was silently burning everything down at home.
Another person pacing a grocery store at night because being alone with their thoughts felt dangerous.

Different lives. Same mechanics.

Each got an hour.
Each got a plan.
Each got one instruction afterward:

Text me once this week with **survived** or **struggled**.

Not because I'm checking up on you.
Because momentum is built through contact, not intention.

Who This Actually Works For

This doesn't work for everyone.

Not because they're bad people.
Because their loop isn't ready to be retrained.

If you want to vent, I'm not your guy.
If you want motivation, go scroll.
If you want someone to hold your hand while you keep doing the same shit, pass.

This works for people who are exhausted by their own patterns.

People who are capable. Smart. Responsible.
And still can't reliably do the thing they said they would do.

People who don't need more insight — they need fewer decisions when their nervous system is under load.

I help people who are standing inside the loop, not theorizing about it.

Because relevance beats brilliance every time.

If I've stood where you're standing, I can help you build something that holds.
If I haven't, I won't pretend.

This isn't about being special.
It's about being precise.

The One-Page Medicine

Here's the part people miss:

Insight doesn't change behavior under pressure.

Systems do.

The plan has to fit on one page.
If it can't be photographed and pulled up when your brain is already offline, it's useless.

These plans aren't pretty. They're functional.
Napkins. Receipts. Index cards. Whatever's nearby.

Because when the loop activates, aesthetics don't matter.
Survival does.

Here's an actual plan I wrote for someone whose evenings kept detonating their progress:

FRIDAY NIGHT PLAN (When the Loop Shows Up)

5:00 PM
Change clothes. Leave the house immediately.
Do not sit. Do not scroll. Do not "just check one thing."
Movement breaks the loop. Stillness feeds it.

5:15 PM
Call a human while walking.
One person. If they don't answer, call the next.
No deciding. Someone answers.

6:00 PM
Same food. Same order. Every time.
Decision fatigue is not a mindset issue. It's a nervous system issue.

7:00 PM
Structured environment. Start time. Other people.
Somewhere your absence would be noticed.

8:30 PM
Hot shower. Long. Intentional.
This is a transition ritual. Not self-care. A reset.

9:00 PM
Phone out of reach. Familiar noise on.
Nothing new. Nothing activating.
Your brain needs predictability, not stimulation.

10:30 PM
Horizontal. Dark. Even if sleep doesn't come.
Tomorrow is easier if tonight doesn't get fucked.

RED FLAGS THAT CHANGE THE PLAN

- Passing a known trigger → Call immediately.
- Old message hits → Screenshot. Don't respond.
- The silence spikes → Go somewhere public, even if you sit in the car.

That's it.

Not inspiring.
Not profound.

Reliable.

And reliability is what retrains the loop.

The Courthouse Bench Moment

Sometimes I don't plan this.
The moment shows up anyway.

Like the person sitting outside a courtroom, hands shaking, brain racing, about to blow the whole thing by saying too much.

I didn't give a speech.

I handed them an index card:

Breathe 4–4–4–4.
Answer only what's asked.
Facts. Not feelings.
You're here to be steady, not impressive.

They read it until their name was called.

Later I got a text:
"I didn't spiral. It went better than expected."

That's what a system does.

It gives you something to stand on when your internal world is chaos.

When This Goes Sideways

I fuck this up.

I've given time to people who didn't want change — just permission.
I've built plans for people who wanted relief, not responsibility.
I've watched someone use a survival system to justify staying in the loop.

That one hurt.

I wanted to control the outcome.
Make sure they used it "right."

That's just my addiction to control wearing a helper mask.

I can build the system.
I can't run it for you.

And if you need me to, you're not ready yet.

The Boundary Part Nobody Likes

Here's the truth:

Momentum dies without boundaries.

Early on, I made myself available all the time.
Middle-of-the-night texts. Crisis calls. Emotional dumping.

I was wrecked.
My life was worse.
And I was closer to blowing everything up.

Now it's clean:

One hour.
One plan.
One check-in.

Because structure protects both of us.

Here's the script I use. Exactly:

"I can help you build a system for your hardest window. We'll do it in one hour. I'll check in once. After that, you run it. If you need ongoing support, I know places that do that. This is what I offer. Want it?"

No negotiation.
No rescuing.

Boundaries aren't cold.
They're what make momentum possible.

The Compound Interest of Being Useful

I've done this every Thursday for two years.

Here's the math:

52 weeks × 1 person = 52 moments where someone didn't implode.

But that's surface level.

The real return is this:

Every system I help someone build reinforces my own.
Every plan I write makes my next hard moment easier.
Every **survived** text is proof that reliability can be trained.

This is how the loop gets retrained.

Not by white-knuckling.
Not by wanting it more.

By building systems that work when you don't.

That's Reliable Momentum.

And once you feel it — once forward motion becomes predictable — you stop asking "what's wrong with me?"

You already know the answer.

Nothing.

You just needed something that holds.

The Text That Changed Everything

Six months into Service Sprints. 11:07 PM. My phone lights up:

"I'm parked outside Rosie's. Tell me not to go in."

I know this guy. Helped him five weeks ago. Thought he was solid. I call immediately, no text back.

"Hey man."

"I'm so fucking close to going in."

"Engine on. Right now."

I hear the engine turn.

"We're driving to Walmart. You're going to buy bananas and Gatorade. I'm staying on the phone. Drive."

"This is stupid."

"Stupid and sober beats smart and drunk. Drive."

Fifteen minutes later, he's laughing in the produce section, holding bananas, telling me about the look the clerk gave him. Crisis redirected into comedy.

Saturday text: "Survived. Bought more bananas. It's a thing now."

He's eight months sober now. Still buys bananas when the urge hits. Still texts "survived" on Saturdays.

Your Service Sprint Starter

Want to try this? Start small. Smaller than you think.

Look around your actual life—not Instagram, not the internet, your actual life. Who's drowning in the exact water you learned to swim in? Who's fighting the exact fight you survived last year?

Pick one person. Offer one hour. Share one tool that actually worked for you. Not theory. Not what should work. What actually kept you from drowning on your worst Tuesday.

Write it ugly on whatever's handy. Hand it over like it's medicine, because it is. Check in once, then let them run it.

That's it. That's the whole system.

The Permission Slip Nobody Gave Me

You don't need to be fully healed to help. If that was the requirement, nobody would help anybody. You just need to be one page ahead of someone who's drowning.

You don't need credentials. Your pain is your credential. Your survival is your certification. Your Thursday night system is someone else's salvation.

You don't need a platform. You need a receipt and a pen. You need an hour and a phone number. You need to remember what drowning felt like and be willing to throw a rope.

Stop waiting to be worthy of service. You became worthy the moment you survived something someone else is facing right now.

The Truth About Day 401

Day 401 is when I stopped counting days and started counting people. Not because days don't matter—they do. Every single one. But because people matter more. Because every person I help is another reason to make it to Day 402.

Recovery alone is survival. I did that for 400 days. White-knuckled through birthdays and holidays and Fridays and court dates. Survived, but barely.

Recovery with purpose is a life. That started on Day 401, in a grocery store, with a receipt and a shaking dad who just needed someone to tell him that 5 PM doesn't have to mean vodka.

You didn't get sober to be safe. Safe is important, but it's not enough. You got sober to be useful. To take your specific mess and turn it into someone else's map. To prove that drowning isn't permanent if someone throws you a rope.

This Thursday, help one person. One hour. One page. One specific tool that worked when you were dying. Don't make it pretty. Make it real. Make it useful. Make it something they can photograph and pull up at 11:07 PM in a bar parking lot.

Then watch what happens to your own recovery when you become necessary to someone else's.

You're not a savior. You're not a guru. You're just someone who survived Thursday and can show someone else how.

That's enough. That's everything.

Now go be useful. One ugly receipt at a time.

Part 1 — The Heretic's Playbook: When Everything Else Fails

9:47 PM. Laptop open. A DM thread blinking at me like an old dealer's number.

The sender's name alone made my chest tight. Someone from the before times. Someone who knew the version of me that stayed up until 4 AM chasing dopamine in all the wrong neighborhoods. The message preview showed just enough: "Hey stranger, remember when we..."

My body was already tilting toward it. That familiar lean that happens in the three seconds before a bad decision. The one where your shoulders round forward and your breathing gets shallow and some ancient part of your brain whispers "just peek."

This is where I used to lose three hours. Where I'd start with "just checking" and end with seventeen tabs open, heart racing, 12:47 AM on the clock, hating myself for falling for the same trick again.

But not tonight. Because now I have a playbook. Not a perfect system. Not a motivational framework. Just four moves I can run in under three minutes when my better angels are off duty.

The Loop That Saved My Ass

5-4-3-2-1. I counted down and stood up before my brain could make a case for staying. Walked to the hallway. Docked the phone. The laptop stayed in the office.

That's move one: **Five Seconds**. Start moving before negotiation begins.

Then I texted my accountability buddy: "Wobble. Docked phone. Two minutes of breathing." No essay. No context. Just the truth in nine words.

That's move two: **Honest Inch**. Tell one small truth and move one inch in the right direction.

In my daily note, I wrote: "9:49 PM - docked. DM trigger. Breathing. Text sent."

Move three: **Receipts**. Evidence that I did the thing.

Next morning, during coffee, I spent two minutes reviewing: What was the trigger? Fatigue plus nostalgia. What's the pattern? Always between 9:30 and 10 PM when I'm alone with the laptop. What's one tweak? Add an 11-minute wind-down at 9:15 - stretch, wash face, read one page of a paper book.

Move four: **Review**. Learn, don't prosecute.

The whole loop took 2 minutes and 47 seconds. The urge passed in less than five. I went to bed clean instead of wired. That's the whole playbook.

Why This Works When Nothing Else Does

Here's what nobody tells you about behavior change: It's not about discipline. It's not about wanting it bad enough. It's about having a system so simple you can run it when you're exhausted, triggered, and three seconds from making the same mistake you've made a hundred times before.

The Heretic's Playbook works because it's built for your worst moment, not your best. When you're sharp and motivated, you don't need a playbook. You need it at 9:47 PM when you're tired and lonely and that familiar itch is promising relief it never actually delivers.

Most recovery systems are built for Sunday morning when you're caffeinated and hopeful. This one's built for Thursday night when you're depleted and nobody's watching.

Five Seconds: The Negotiation Killer

Your brain is a negotiation machine. Give it six seconds and it'll build a compelling case for why this time is different. Why you've earned it. Why you can handle it. Why it's actually self-care.

Five seconds short-circuits the debate. 5-4-3-2-1 and you're moving before the committee in your head can file an objection.

I learned this the hard way. January 2024, trying to break my phone habit. I'd tell myself "Don't check Instagram" and then spend twenty minutes debating whether checking Instagram was really that bad. By minute twenty-one, I'd already checked it.

The breakthrough came when I stopped debating and started moving. 5-4-3-2-1, phone in the dock. No discussion. No negotiation. Just physics— object in motion stays in motion.

Real Five Second Moves That Actually Work

Night scroll urge: 5-4-3-2-1, stand up, phone in hallway dock, bathroom, brush teeth. By the time you're done, the urge has usually passed.

Work avoidance at 10:30 AM: 5-4-3-2-1, open the document, type three terrible sentences. Momentum beats perfection every time.

Conflict heat rising with Kelly: 5-4-3-2-1, close mouth, breathe (4 seconds in, 2 hold, 8 out), say "I'm defensive. Give me ten minutes." Those ten minutes have saved my marriage more than any therapy session.

Gas station at 6:15 PM: 5-4-3-2-1, turn wheel toward exit, call buddy while driving, stay on until you're home. The urge can't survive a conversation.

Kitchen raid at 10 PM: 5-4-3-2-1, glass of water, planned snack (the one you put at eye level earlier), brush teeth. Make the right thing easier than the wrong thing.

The key is to make the action so small it's embarrassing. Don't run a mile. Stand up. Don't write the chapter. Open the document. Don't have the hard conversation. Send a two-word text: "Thinking. Tomorrow?"

Honest Inch: The Anti-Perfection Protocol

Perfection is procrastination in a tuxedo. It keeps you planning the perfect recovery while you're actively drowning. The Honest Inch says: Tell one ugly truth and move one inch in the right direction. That's it.

"I want to check her Instagram" becomes "I'm going to walk around the block instead."

"I'm avoiding the draft because I'm scared it'll suck" becomes three shitty sentences typed.

"I was short with you" becomes "Sorry. I was wrong."

One truth. One inch. No heroics.

Last Tuesday, 2:15 PM. Classic danger zone—post-lunch fog, nobody home, laptop open. The urge to "just check something" arrived right on schedule. Old me would've either white-knuckled through it or folded completely.

New me did an Honest Inch: Opened my notes app and typed "I want to scroll because I'm bored and under-stimulated." Then did fifteen pushups. Took forty seconds. Urge died. Went back to work.

That's not inspiring. It's not Instagram-worthy. But it works.

Receipts: Your Brain Lies, Timestamps Don't

Your memory is a creative writing exercise. By Friday, your brain will have edited the week into whatever story supports your current mood. If you feel like a failure, it'll delete every win. If you feel invincible, it'll minimize every wobble.

Receipts don't lie. They're boring, factual proof that you did the thing.

"10:47 AM - opened doc, wrote 3 bullets"
"2:15 PM - pushups instead of scroll"
"9:49 PM - docked, texted J"

Not a journal. Not processing. Just timestamps and facts. Takes ten seconds. Changes everything.

I keep mine in a note called "Done" because that's all I'm tracking—what got done. Not feelings. Not insights. Just evidence that I'm someone who does what he says he'll do, even when he doesn't feel like it.

Review: Two Minutes to Not Repeat History

Every night, before the phone dock, I spend two minutes scanning the receipts. Not prosecuting myself. Not building a case. Just asking:

- What worked?
- Where did it wobble?
- What's one tweak?

That's it. Two minutes. Usually while brushing my teeth.

Last week's review: Three wobbles, all between 9:30-10 PM, all when alone with laptop. Tweak: Laptop gets docked at 9:15 PM next to the phone. Problem solved? We'll see. But at least I'm running experiments instead of repeating loops.

Friday gets ten minutes. Same questions, wider lens. Looking for patterns, not problems. The data tells me things my feelings won't: Most wobbles happen when I skip morning workout. Service Sprint prevents Thursday night spirals. Every "just five minutes" becomes forty-five.

The Ugly Truth About What Works

This system isn't sexy. It's not going viral on TikTok. It's not even particularly clever. It's just four things you can do when you're about to do the wrong thing:

Count down and move. Tell the truth and inch forward. Write it down. Learn from it.

That's the whole playbook. It's heretical because it doesn't promise transformation. It promises to get you through the next five minutes without making things worse. Stack enough five-minute wins and you get a different life. Not a perfect life. A present one.

Tonight's Practice

Tonight, when you feel the pull toward whatever your thing is—the scroll, the site, the substance, the spiral—run the loop:

5-4-3-2-1 and move your body away from the trigger.

Text someone the truth in under ten words.

Write down what you did with a timestamp.

Tomorrow morning, spend two minutes asking what you learned.

That's it. That's the whole assignment. Not forever. Just tonight. Just these four moves.

Because the secret to recovery isn't perfection. It's having something you can do at 9:47 PM when perfection is off the table and all you've got is five seconds to choose between the loop that kills you and the loop that saves you.

Choose the boring loop. It leads somewhere better.

Part 2 — The 30-Day Practice Plan (Or: How to Actually Do This)

Here's the thing about systems: They're worthless without reps. You can understand the playbook perfectly and still be scrolling at midnight wondering where three hours went. The difference between knowing and doing is practice. Boring, repetitive, unsexy practice.

So here's a month of it. Not because 30 days is magic. Because it's long enough to feel the difference and short enough that your brain won't panic.

The Daily Loop (Under 5 Minutes, Because You're Busy Lying to Yourself)

Morning (30 seconds): First thing after your eyes open—before the phone, before the scroll, before your brain starts its bullshit—5-4-3-2-1 and start your first real action. Make the bed. Fill the water bottle. Open the document. Whatever you decided last night. Just start it.

Then read your clarity sentence from Chapter 15. Mine this week: "I choose presence over performance." Yours will be different. Make it short enough to remember, true enough to sting.

Midday (2 minutes): That thing you're avoiding? The email, the call, the conversation? Do an Honest Inch on it. Not the whole thing. Just one inch. Send the subject line. Dial the number and hang up (counts). Walk to the room where the conversation needs to happen.

I know this sounds pathetic. That's the point. Pathetic inches beat heroic paralysis.

Evening (2 minutes): Before the phone dock, two quick receipts:

- What got started?

- What inch got moved?

Then the review—while brushing your teeth because you're going to brush them anyway:

- One win (can be tiny).
- One wobble (just name it).
- One tweak (make it specific).

Example from last Tuesday:

- Win: Didn't check email until noon.
- Wobble: 2:30 PM scroll hole (12 minutes).
- Tweak: Tomorrow, set a 2:25 PM alarm for pushups.

That's the whole daily loop. Five minutes total. Less time than you spend debating whether to check Instagram.

The Weekly Architecture

Monday: Set your HPH Sprint from Chapter 15. What's the One Thing that moves your real work forward this week? Not ten things. One. Mine this week: Draft three chapters. Yours might be: Have the money conversation. Fix the resume. Call Mom.

Thursday: Service Sprint from Chapter 16. Text one person who might be struggling. Offer one specific help. Don't wait for the perfect moment or the perfect words. "Thinking of you. Can I grab your groceries?" beats a paragraph of poetry.

Friday: Ten-minute weekly review. Count your receipts. Look for patterns. Celebrate the boring wins—they're the ones that compound.

What to Actually Track (The Only Numbers That Matter)

Forget complex metrics. Track three things:

1. Consistency: Did you run the loop today? Yes = 1, No = 0. That's it. No partial credit. No "kind of." Binary scoring because your brain needs clarity.

2. Urges Averted: Every time you 5-4-3-2-1 away from your thing, mark it. I use tally marks in my notebook. You might use a counter app. Don't overthink it. Just count.

3. Service Done: Did you do your Thursday sprint? Y/N.

That's all. Not mood. Not energy. Not productivity. Just: Did you do the simple thing you said you'd do?

The Urge Tracking That Actually Helps

Most people track triggers wrong. They write novels about their feelings. They psychoanalyze their childhood. They create complex spreadsheets that they abandon by day four.

Here's what works:

The Tally + Trigger Method: Make a mark every time you avert an urge. Next to it, write 2-3 words max:

- | | | | 2:30 PM bored
- | | | | 9:45 PM lonely
- | | | | traffic angry
- | | | | Kelly argument

After a week, patterns jump out. Oh look, every wobble happens between 2-3 PM or after 9:30 PM. Now you can plan for it.

Last month, my pattern was embarrassingly clear: Eight marks between 2-3 PM, all "bored" or "tired." Solution: Scheduled 2:15 PM walks. Wobbles dropped 70%. Not because I became disciplined. Because I stopped being surprised.

The Design Kit That Keeps You Honest

In Your Wallet: A card that says:

- Front: "5-4-3-2-1 → Truth → Receipt → Review".
- Back: Three names with phone numbers—people who answer when you're drowning.

Mine has my sponsor, my buddy James, and Kelly. Yours needs people who won't judge but won't enable. People who'll answer at 10 PM with "Come over" or "Meet me at Starbucks."

On Your Phone:

- 9:15 PM alarm: "Start wind-down".
- 2:25 PM alarm: "Danger zone - move your body".
- A note called "Done" for receipts.
- Focus mode that blocks your triggers during hot zones.

In Your Space:

- Phone dock visible from your bed (seeing it empty helps).
- Tomorrow's clarity sentence on the bathroom mirror.
- Your running shoes by the door (easier to run than to move them).

The Relapse Contingency (Because Hope Isn't a Strategy)

Let's talk about what nobody wants to talk about: What to do when you fail? Not if. When. Because if you're human and fighting something real, you're going to have days where the playbook doesn't hold.

The First 30 Minutes After You Fold:

1. 5-4-3-2-1 and physically move to a different room.
2. Drink a full glass of water (dehydration makes everything worse).
3. Text your person: "Slipped. Safe. Calling in 5."
4. Do something physical for 60 seconds—jumping jacks, cold water on face, step outside.
5. Call your person and say what happened in three sentences, no more.

The Next 24 Hours:

- No big decisions.
- No dramatic confessions on social media.
- No punishment workouts.
- No isolating in shame.
- One small win within 2 hours (make bed, take shower, eat real food).
- Back to the basic loop immediately.

What Actually Happens When You Slip:

October 2024. Had sixty-three days clean from late-night scrolling. Thursday night, Kelly and I had an argument about money. She went to bed hurt. I stayed up to "work."

10:15 PM: Opened laptop to finish a proposal.
10:17 PM: "Just checking" email.
10:22 PM: "Somehow" on Instagram.
11:45 PM: Still scrolling, eyes burning, shame growing.
12:20 AM: Finally closed laptop, hating myself.

The old me would've turned this into a three-day spiral. "You failed, might as well keep going." But I ran the contingency:

Texted James: "Scrolled 2 hours. Done. Talking tomorrow."

Drank water, did pushups until my arms shook.

Set phone and laptop in garage (extreme but necessary).

Morning: told Kelly the truth, apologized for both things.

Back to the loop at 6 AM.

The slip became data: Arguments are triggers. Need a protocol for conflict nights. Now when we argue, devices go in the dock before bed, no exceptions. Haven't had a post-argument scroll since.

Week-by-Week What to Expect

Week 1: You'll be excited and probably perfect for three days. Day 4-5, the novelty wears off. You'll forget the evening review. You'll remember at 11 PM and feel like a failure. Do it anyway, even at 11 PM. Especially at 11 PM.

Week 2: The resistance shows up. Your brain starts negotiating. "This is stupid." "It's not working." "I don't need structure." This is exactly when you need it most. Keep going. Make the receipts even shorter if you need to. But keep going.

Week 3: Something shifts. The loop becomes automatic. You're 5-4-3-2-1ing without thinking about it. The evening review happens while you're brushing your teeth. You might have your first "holy shit, this is working" moment. Don't get cocky. The system is working, not you.

Week 4: You'll either get sloppy because it's working or rigid because you're afraid to break the streak. Both are wrong. Stay boring. Stay consistent. The magic isn't in perfection—it's in repetition.

Three True Stories from the Loop

The Gas Station Save: Day 18, driving home from a brutal client meeting. The gas station on Route 9 calling my name. Not for gas. For the old ritual. Five seconds: 5-4-3-2-1, called James, stayed on while I drove past, went to a different station two miles away. Receipt: "5:47 PM - called instead of stopped." That call saved more than my evening.

The 2 AM Truth: Week 3, couldn't sleep. 2:13 AM. Everyone says don't make decisions at 2 AM, but the urge to scroll was screaming. Honest Inch: Texted my accountability group: "Can't sleep. Want to scroll. Getting up to read paper book instead." Three guys texted back within minutes. We're all fighting the same fights at 2 AM.

The Friday That Clicked: Week 4, Friday review showed eleven averted urges, all successful. Not because I'm strong. Because I finally had something to do besides white-knuckle through them. The playbook gave me moves when I needed moves, not motivation.

Your First 30 Days Start Now

Not Monday. Not January 1st. Not after you feel ready. Now. Tonight. With whatever energy you have left.

Before you go to bed:

1. Write your clarity sentence on paper.
2. Put it where you'll see it tomorrow.
3. Set your 9:15 PM wind-down alarm.
4. Pick your first Five Second morning action.
5. Text one person: "Starting something. Will need you. Details tomorrow."

That's five minutes. You have five minutes. You spend more time scrolling reviews for things you'll never buy.

The Boring Truth That Changes Everything

This system isn't going to make you extraordinary. It's going to make you reliable. You're going to become someone who does what they say they'll do, even when they don't feel like it. Even at 9:47 PM. Even when triggered. Even when tired.

That's not sexy. It's not viral. It's just true.

And after 30 days of boring consistency, you'll have something you haven't had in years: evidence that you can trust yourself. Not faith. Not hope. Evidence. Receipts. Proof that when you say you'll do something, you do it.

That changes everything. Not overnight. Not dramatically. Just steadily, boringly, one Five Second decision at a time.

The loop is waiting. Your move.

5-4-3-2-1.

Start.

CHAPTER 18

The Proof is in the Ordinary Joy

May 2025. Same hibachi restaurant. Same onion volcano. Same chef making the same joke about catching shrimp in your mouth. But this time, I see it all.

The chef lights the onion tower and my youngest daughter's eyes go wide—not because it's her first time, but because fire is always magic when you're eleven. My teenage daughter films it for her friends, narrating with that specific teenage mix of excitement and irony. Kelly's hand finds mine across the table, not checking my pulse, just holding it.

I'm here. Actually here. Not managing myself through dinner. Not counting minutes until escape. Not performing presence while planning my exit. Just here, watching my kid fail spectacularly at catching flying shrimp, laughing hard enough that my sides hurt.

Years ago at this same table, I was underwater. Phone hidden in my lap like contraband, thumb working while my face pretended to care. Every laugh calculated. Every response delayed by the three-second buffer of a man trying to appear normal while drowning. My family had learned to work around my absence—conversations flowing past me like I was furniture that happened to eat.

Tonight, my phone is in the car. Not because of a rule. Because I forgot about it.

That's when you know the architecture worked.

The Math Nobody Explains

Here's what the recovery books don't tell you: The goal isn't to become extraordinary. It's to become capable of receiving ordinary joy without needing to enhance, escape, or document it. To sit through a mundane Tuesday dinner without your skin trying to crawl off your body.

Every protocol in this book—every Truth Culture conversation at 2 AM when I wanted to lie, every steelmanned urge at 11:47 PM when my hand reached for the phone, every deep work block I protected like a child, every Friday Night Planning session I didn't want to do—it all led here. To this table. To the choice to watch my kid miss her mouth with flying rice and find it hilarious instead of checking the time.

My older daughter says, "Dad, remember when you taught me that breathing thing before my presentation?"

She's talking about something from last month, not last year. We have recent memories now. Fresh inventory. Current stock. Not the yellowed receipts of a father who was physically present but mentally AWOL.

"The box breathing? Yeah, did you use it?"

"Every time. Even before Jason asked me out."

Her sister spits her water. "JASON ASKED YOU OUT?"

And we're off—a normal family conversation about normal family things. Nobody's managing me. Nobody's checking if I'm okay. Nobody's doing that careful dance around Dad's mood. I'm just Dad, present and accounted for, ready to terrorize my daughter about her boyfriend with the appropriate amount of father energy.

This is what I got sober for. Not for the big moments. For this stupid, perfect Tuesday.

The Invisible Architecture

The systems that saved my life are still running, but they're quiet now. Like breathing. You don't think about breathing until you can't.

Truth Culture happens every Sunday after dinner but it's just five minutes now. "What's real this week?" Everyone answers. Nobody cries anymore. It's maintenance, not surgery.

Physical Intelligence still means I train six days a week. 5:47 AM alarm. Gym by 6:15. Sometimes Livvie joins me, doing curls with the 5-pound dumbbells while informing me she needs to be stronger than the "stupid boys" in 7th grade who think they own the basketball court. I don't tell her she's already stronger than most adults I know—not in her arms, but in her certainty that she deserves space.

Deep Work blocks still live in my calendar—9 AM to noon, phone in another room, door closed, single task only. But now they end with me actually closing my laptop. Actually transitioning. Not sneaking in "just five more minutes" that become forty-five.

The architecture became invisible because it became life. That's the goal. Not to be someone who uses recovery tools, but someone who doesn't need to think about them anymore because they're just how you live.

At 7:47 PM—I know the exact time because I'm present enough to notice—our chef does the volcano trick where he squirts sake into the fire. Everyone at our table leans back and goes "Ohhhhh" in unison like we're watching fireworks. I catch Kelly's eye. She's smiling at me with that specific smile that means she's happy, not monitoring. There's a difference. After two years, I know the difference.

"What?" I ask.

"Nothing. You're just... here."

Three words that cost me three years to earn.

The Compound Effect of Showing Up

Two years of deposits that looked like nothing while they were happening. Saturday afternoons playing Monopoly where I learned my youngest palms cards when she's bluffing—left hand to her chest, every time. Tuesday homework sessions where my older daughter revealed she's secretly brilliant at math but hides it because smart isn't cool in 9th grade. Wednesday walks with Kelly where we stopped talking about who's picking up groceries and started talking about what we're building. The ritual where everyone shares their "peak and pit" from the day— stolen from some parenting blog Kelly found, but it works.

Friday afternoon pickups where being the reliable parent sometimes just means making sure SOMEBODY gets Livvie from school. Last week it was

Kelly because I had a client emergency. But I arranged it. I communicated it. I didn't just not show up and hope someone would figure it out. That's the difference between recovery and whatever I was doing before.

None of these moments were Instagram-worthy. Nobody would watch the movie of me helping with algebra homework or sitting through a dance recital without checking my phone. But stack them up—a thousand tiny Tuesday moments—and you get a life. A real one. Not the highlight reel. The actual life.

Recovery math is simple: 1,000 ordinary moments > 1 extraordinary moment. Because life is mostly Tuesday at 6:30 PM, deciding what's for dinner. And if you can't be present for Tuesday, you're missing 80% of your existence.

From Debt to Dividends

My youngest asks if we can get dessert. Years ago, this would have triggered the whole cascade: mental math about money, shame about the mental math, the need to escape the shame, the phone appearing in my hand like magic.

Tonight, I just say yes. Not because we're rich—we're not. But because I'm not spending $500 a month on numbing agents. Because I didn't lose three clients last year to unreliability. Because when you're actually present, you stop bleeding money on things that promise to make you feel better but leave you feeling nothing.

We order fried ice cream. It comes out on fire because this is hibachi and everything must be on fire. My teenager takes seventeen photos. My youngest tries to eat it while it's still flaming because she has no survival instinct. Kelly steals bites from everyone's plate while denying she's doing it. I sit back and watch my family be a family.

This is what being addicted to the right things looks like. Not perfect. Not performed. Just present. Just here. Just this table with these specific humans who somehow still want me around.

The Secret Sunday Game

Every Sunday after dinner, we play a game. Nobody knows it's a recovery tool. Nobody knows it's keeping me sober. They just know Dad asks weird questions and everyone has to answer.

"What ordinary thing felt good this week?"

My youngest goes first because she always goes first: "When you helped me with free throws and didn't try to fix my form even though it was killing you."

My teenager, looking at her phone but still participating: "Wednesday when we just sat in the car listening to music after school and you didn't ask me about my day."

Kelly: "Thursday morning when you brought me coffee without me asking. With the good creamer."

Me: "Right now. This conversation. Even though Emmy's on her phone."

"I'm listening!" Emmy protests, not looking up.

Second question: "When did you catch yourself totally here this week?"

The answers are never big. Walking the dog and noticing the neighbor's new fence. Washing dishes together and everyone singing that stupid song from that stupid commercial. The moment in a movie when everyone laughed at the same dumb joke at the same time. That's the point. Joy lives in the mundane. Recovery is learning to receive it without needing to enhance it.

Last question: "What small thing should we do next week?"

Not vacation planning. Not life goals. Just: Make tacos Tuesday. Try that new ice cream place. Have a Mario Kart tournament where Dad doesn't let anyone win. Ordinary plans that give us something to look toward without needing to escape toward it.

This isn't therapy. It's a five-minute conversation that reminds us what we're building and why. It trains our attention to hunt for joy in its everyday clothes instead of waiting for it to show up in a tuxedo.

What Victory Actually Looks Like

The check comes. I pay it without the mental gymnastics—the calculating, the justifying, the promising myself we'll eat ramen for a week. We walk to the car, my youngest racing ahead to call shotgun even though she knows she can't sit in front. My teenager and Kelly debating whether that one song is about a breakup or death. I'm not analyzing any of this. I'm not making it mean something. I'm just walking behind my family, watching their shadows stretch under parking lot lights, feeling the specific weight of keys in my pocket, hearing their voices bounce off cars.

Years ago—no, be specific—October 2023, I would have been calculating how many hours until I could be alone with my habits. Managing myself through the presence performance until I could drop the act. Using the bathroom twice during dinner just to check my phone. Coming back to conversations I'd missed the beginning of, faking my way through responses.

Tonight, I'm planning nothing. There's nowhere I'd rather be than this parking lot with these people. No enhancement needed. No escape required. Just this walk across asphalt with humans I love.

The thought hits me: This is it. This is the whole point. Not some breakthrough or revelation. Just being able to walk to your car after dinner without wishing you were somewhere else.

The Test Results Are In

Remember that Tuesday in 2023 when I was drowning at the dinner table? When my family operated around my absence like water flowing around a rock? When I was gone but still there?

The test results are in: Recovery worked.

Not because I'm special. I'm not. I'm just another addict who got lucky enough to find the right architecture before I lost everything. The Truth Culture that made lying harder than telling the truth. The steelmanning practice that took the power out of urges by naming them clearly. The deep work blocks that gave me something better than scroll—actual accomplishment. The physical practice that taught me I could do hard things without dying. The service that reminded me other people have real problems while I'm worried about my phone battery.

All of it—every system, every protocol, every awkward conversation at 2 AM—led here. To this parking lot. To this moment where I'm not thinking about the moment but just living in it.

Your Brain is Going to Get Addicted to Something

Let's be clear about something: Your brain doesn't care what you get addicted to. It just wants to repeat what works. The machine is neutral. It will get just as hooked on morning runs as morning scroll. On cold plunges as porn binges. On truth-telling as lying.

So make the right things work.

Get addicted to the feeling after you tell the truth—that specific lightness, like taking off a backpack you forgot you were wearing. Chase the exhaustion after real training, when your hands shake but your mind goes quiet. Hunt for the satisfaction of closing your laptop after three hours of deep work, knowing you actually made something.

Get hooked on the relief of saying "I was wrong" without defending yourself. On the connection when phones are docked and you can see everyone's actual face. On the peace of keeping promises to yourself— small ones, then bigger ones, until reliability becomes your new drug.

Get obsessed with random Tuesday dinners where nothing happens except love.

These addictions compound. They pay dividends. They build instead of burn.

Tonight's Assignment (The Only One That Matters)

Tonight, put your phone in another room. Not forever. Just tonight. Sit with someone you love. If you live alone, sit with yourself—that counts too.

Notice one ordinary thing. How they hold their coffee cup with both hands when it's warm. The way they laugh at their own jokes before they tell them. How they look when they're concentrating—that little furrow between their eyebrows.

Don't document it. Don't enhance it. Don't make it mean something. Just receive it.

That's the whole assignment. The whole point. To be present for the ordinary moments that make an extraordinary life. Not because they're perfect, but because they're real. Not because they're special, but because they're yours.

The math is simple: Every system in this book is worth it if it leads to one real moment of undefended presence with someone you love. Every urge you've steelmanned, every truth you've told, every block you've protected—it all leads to this capacity. To just be here. To just be normal. To just be human without needing to enhance or escape or edit the experience.

The Final Receipt

My youngest buckles her seatbelt and asks, "Can we come back next month?"

"Every month," I say. And I mean it. Not because hibachi is special. Because showing up is.

My teenager puts on her music—something aggressive that Kelly pretends to hate but secretly knows all the words to. Kelly reaches over and squeezes my hand, three pulses—our code for "I love you" when words feel too big. I start the car. We drive home through familiar streets, toward our ordinary house, to our ordinary evening routine. Bath time and homework. Dishes and lunches for tomorrow. Maybe some bad TV if we're not too tired.

Two years ago, this would have felt like prison. Tonight, it feels like freedom.

This is what I got sober for. This is what I stay sober for. This drive home with people I love, fully here, needing nothing more than what this moment is already offering.

You can have this too. Not the same details—your ordinary joy will look different. But the presence. The peace. The ability to receive your life instead of constantly trying to escape it.

The architecture is here. The tools are tested. The path is marked by thousands who've walked it before you, left their breadcrumbs, their blood, their stories.

Your move.

Choose your addictions carefully. Choose the ones that lead you home.

Starting tonight. Starting with putting your phone in another room and seeing what happens when you stop documenting your life and start living it.

The ordinary is waiting. It's been waiting the whole time.

You Shouldn't Be Here — What Writing This Book Actually Cost Me

The house had settled into that late-night stillness where even the HVAC sounded like it was holding a breath, the refrigerator ticking somewhere in the dark kitchen like a metronome only the walls could hear, and the pale, blue-white light of the screen washed across my skin in a way that made me look both present and ghosted at the same time. My fingers hovered over the keys with that strange tension you get when your body thinks it should run but there's nowhere to go, calves tightening as if they remembered something my mind was still pretending not to know.

I could taste old mint and metal—adrenaline always has that copper edge if you've lived with it long enough—and the coffee from earlier had soured into a film at the back of my throat, the kind that lingers even after days like this. My shirt still carried a wisp of detergent, clean in a way that mocked how grimy I felt on the inside, like the outside had followed the instructions and the inside had disobeyed every single one.

I typed the first few letters by muscle memory, the browser greeting me like an old accomplice—autocomplete pulsing up the forbidden doorway before I'd even fully committed. I swallowed. I watched the cursor blink, not neutrally but insistently, like it was tapping its foot, counting down to the thing I wanted to pretend I wasn't already choosing.

I told myself the oldest lie I know how to speak: I'm not here to go all the way. Just a peek. Just enough to release the pressure so I could sleep and wake up tomorrow as the man I advertised—husband, father, performer, provider—someone who hits quotas and remembers birthdays and sends invoices and carries his life like it's solid. I wasn't chasing sex. I was chasing the chemical I had trained myself to need, the one that promised—always falsely—that this time it would be enough.

I hit enter.

The screen flashed once, then collapsed into black.

Four words appeared, stark and bright as a slap:

You shouldn't be here.

Everything inside me tightened at once—shoulders climbing toward my ears, hamstrings knotting like I'd stepped wrong, heat flushing through my face only to disappear in the next breath, replaced by that cold you get when you swerve at the last second and realize afterward how close the impact came. My eyes flicked down the hallway as if guilt had a physical form that might catch me mid-act. Wife asleep. Child asleep. Even the dog, had she lifted her head, would've known.

I should tell you: I installed that blocker. A future version of me trying to throw a lifeline back toward the present. But I didn't expect the message to land like scripture—less technical error, more moral indictment, not denying access so much as stating a truth I'd been avoiding on purpose. My first impulse wasn't gratitude; it was irritation so sharp it felt like anger. *Don't parent me.* Then shame. Then that hollow quiet I'd come to recognize as the edge of truth.

The chair pressed into the backs of my thighs; a draft worked its way around my ankles; my jaw felt locked from clenching. And what hit me hardest was how utterly ordinary the moment was—no dramatic lighting, no swelling music, just a man in the dark confronted by the simplest sentence he'd avoided for years.

I call myself dopamine-dependent now, and that feels clean enough, but back then the sensation was simpler: empty, and convinced I deserved temporary relief from that emptiness. I had trained my brain to sprint toward the fastest spike—powder, pixels, applause, overwork—anything that let me sidestep the quiet. My search history wasn't a curiosity; it was a confession.

That night at the desk was the first scene that wrote back at me. It showed me the loop not as a theory but as a lived architecture I'd been walking blind. And it was that night I understood, truly, what this book would cost—not the time or the effort but the confrontation with memories I had buried under performance.

There's a moment I almost cut every time I passed over it in the draft. Even now, my hands hesitate because memory can be cruel in how it returns—never the whole film, just fragments, outlines, and the scent that won't leave.

Eighteen. One of those nights you tell yourself you're built for, when "fun" masquerades as identity and volume substitutes for belonging, when music rattles your ribs and the lines on the glass table are careless and large, and someone is laughing too loudly and someone is pressed against you in a way you can't quite remember giving permission for, and then everything speeds up—bumps to rails to tunnel vision.

I don't remember the night.
I remember the waking.

Sheets that weren't mine.
A ceiling that looked offended by daylight.
Her back to me like a verdict.

My skin was scraped raw in places no clothing protects. A friction burn under the ribs. A patch on my thigh that burned when the sheet brushed it. My mouth tasted like battery acid mixed with gum. And the smell— god, the smell—sweet-sour, latex, smoke, something chemical, something decaying. I couldn't scrub it off for weeks, carried it into buses and classrooms and diners. I hated the girl beside me not because of anything she'd done but because she reflected me back to myself, and I wasn't ready to look.

There's no revelation in that morning. Only consequence. I made a vow— *never again*—but vows spoken in hangover light are just negotiations with shame, and shame is a poor accountability partner. Years later, after marriage, remarriage, and divorce twice over, I understood the vow wasn't about stopping; it was about hiding better, concealing not the substances or the sites but the architecture of my life built around them.

Writing forced excavation. The pages were a shovel I couldn't put down.

I dug up the first time I recognized an "innocent habit" as a loop— delaying a call not because I was busy but because the rush of last-minute success fed the same circuit; letting emails pile up so the relief of clearing them felt like a hit; dressing compulsion in professional clothing and calling it ambition.

I dug up the lies I'd told people who loved me, the ones that sound reasonable—"I'm tired," "I'm just off," "Work is heavy"—when the truth was radioactive. I ghosted a friend once because he'd started seeing the pattern; he'd begun placing dots I couldn't afford to have connected. He probably still believes the story was about him. It wasn't.

I dug up two marriages, each with its own theme of betrayal written into the margins. Wife One deserved the version of me I performed but didn't possess. Wife Two deserved a partner who could say, "I'm not okay today; help me safeguard us." Instead, I crafted a persona of calm while running my loop in the dark, then showing up in the morning like a martyr with breakfast. This isn't a performance confession—it's inventory. I built lives that made duplicity easy and discovery hard, and I paid in divorce decrees and echoing rooms.

I dug up my work, which had always been a cocktail of talent and sabotage. The thrill of selling what I hadn't built yet, the humiliation of scrambling to deliver, the way procrastination dressed itself up as creativity, the endless need for jackpot energy. Consistency bored me. The crash and the sprint were where I lived.

And then, almost quietly, something shifted. The first time I redirected an urge into something measurable, it was embarrassingly small. I wanted to scroll, and instead I stood up and did fifteen minutes of prospecting. Closed nothing. But I logged it. *12:40–12:55: dialed.* Such a tiny receipt, but it felt like laying the cornerstone of a life I'd only talked about.

The writing itself became a form of exposure therapy, a kind of mental reconsolidation I hadn't known I needed. I would lift a memory into daylight, describe it in unflinching detail, and return it to the shelf with a new tag: *this is what happened, and here's what it means now.* Each paragraph was a rep. Awkward at first, then steady.

Let me be clear: this wasn't catharsis meant to absolve me. Some people confess to escape consequence; I wrote to confront it. When I revisited that eighteen-year-old morning, I didn't redeem it with soft edges. When

I wrote about the blocker message, I didn't congratulate myself for installing it; I questioned why I needed digital guardrails to keep me from myself.

It cost me. Some days I'd finish a section and feel like I'd been breathing exhaust, the mental haze so thick I couldn't think straight. My body reacted—tight ribs, shallow breath, that familiar hum in the nervous system. I found myself lying on the floor some afternoons with my palms on my chest counting inhales like it was the first time I'd tried. And there were mornings I avoided opening the document because I knew exactly which version of me waited inside, and I didn't like him.

The fear had names. Wife One might read this. Wife Two might read this. Friends I vanished on might finally see it wasn't their failure but mine. And beneath all that sat a quieter fear: being understood. If hatred is blunt, understanding is surgical. It leaves you without shadows.

So, I built guardrails. Brendon drilled into me that design beats discipline, and at the High Performance Institute I finally believed him. I blocked the sites everywhere—not as virtue but as strategy. I banished my phone from the bedroom and bought a cheap alarm clock. I wrote in sprints, used a stop word—"mercy"—when the tension spiked, walked the block after heavy scenes, scheduled therapy like a revenue meeting.

And I kept receipts. PQOs became the ballast against shame. If the writing gutted me at nine, I ensured something was shipped or logged by ten. Not distraction—evidence. Balance.

Then came the shift I didn't see coming.
Halfway through the manuscript, certain memories lost their voltage. Shame dissolved faster, its half-life shortening with each honest paragraph. After finishing Chapter Ten—*Early Recovery*—I closed the laptop and slept a clean, uninterrupted, body-deep sleep, the kind I hadn't tasted in years. It felt like my nervous system finally exhaled.

The body followed. Guilt left in waves, not dramatic ones, more like humidity lifting from asphalt. Tears came unexpectedly—not performative but involuntary. And instead of analyzing them, I let them move through and kept writing.

My life changed shape alongside the work. I'd spent years avoiding places that triggered recognition, living like a fugitive of my own past, constantly scanning for cover. The writing reversed the polarity. I went looking—not for punishment, but for witness. I reread old messages and saw how I apologized without admitting anything. I stood outside bars that held old stories and let the night pass without going in. And I texted a friend I'd abandoned years earlier, explaining the truth he deserved long ago. His response—"I figured something was up. I forgive you."—made me sit in my car and say "Okay" three times, like I needed to prove to the air I could receive it.

Not everything was repaired, and that wasn't the point. Some doors stay closed. Some apologies expire. The goal was to stop lying—first inward, then outward, then on the page. Witness-first repair: rebuild trust with yourself by making your actions visible, countable, repeatable.

People who haven't lived inside loops call this melodrama. Those who have know the currency of the ordinary—a night's sleep without a secret, a day without bargaining, a coffee that doesn't have to rinse out the guilt. These are riches.

High Performance gave me levers. Brendon pushed the questions I hated at the moments I needed them. What are you after? Why does it matter? How will you know you actually did it? He reframed clarity, energy, necessity, productivity, influence, courage—not as ideals, but as disciplines you practice until they become the architecture of your day.

Under that mentorship, writing stopped being a confessional booth and became training. Dopamine isn't a villain; it's a dog that follows your cues. I'd been pointing mine at hiding spots. I began pointing it at outcomes— one more call, one more paragraph, one more honest conversation. Design made the right choice the path of least resistance; discipline shifted from white-knuckling to rhythm.

Part of me still flinches imagining the women I married reading this. Part of me wants to edit toward innocence. But every time I softened a truth to appear better, the book flattened. And every time I named something exactly as it happened, something in me came alive with a precision I didn't know I was capable of.

Here's the part I never expected: writing about addiction made me feel larger, not smaller. The traits I thought disqualified me—obsession, sensitivity, intensity—became instruments when aimed correctly. The impulses that once burned bridges built them. The shame that constricted my throat became permission for others.

I resisted writing that eighteen-year-old memory because I feared disgust. I kept it because disgust was the thing I hadn't faced. Darkness distorts everything. Daylight does the opposite. We find ourselves not by curating our best moments but by standing fully inside the worst ones and deciding what grows there next.

So yes, this book drained me. But it was also the cleanest therapy I've ever done. It forced me to stop treating cravings like clever roommates and start treating them like signals. It forced me to stop letting shame negotiate the terms. It forced me to say things I'd swallowed for decades and realize they didn't kill me. It forced me to admit I'd trained my addictions like racehorses—and that I could train them differently.

If you're reading this because your loops are loud, good. You shouldn't be on the edge of your life bargaining with your own mind in the dark. You should be in the center of it, redirecting the same chemicals toward the work that makes you proud at night. You should be building receipts that can't be argued with. You should be designing a world where truth is easier than secrecy. You should be watching shame evaporate under the heat of honesty.

And if you're afraid the people you hurt will finally understand— welcome. Let them. Not so the weight transfers onto them, but so you can carry your portion and move forward. Forgiveness is optional. Honesty is not.

I return often to that night at the desk. The blocker spoke a sentence I'd outsourced. I needed that then. But I don't need the machine anymore. I can feel the urge rise, feel the old electricity flicker through my fingers, and I can name the truth myself, out loud if necessary:

You shouldn't be here.

Not in the dark bargaining.
Not in rooms that smell like forgetting.
Not in lives built to hide.

You should be here—in the work, in the conversation, in the bed where you actually sleep. At the table in the morning with your child, drinking coffee that doesn't have to erase anything. In your body without apology. In your purpose—not as branding, but as practice: tell the truth, aim the dopamine, design the world, deliver the receipts, repair what you can.

That's where I found myself.
That's where I remain.
Not cured—trained.
Not redeemed—responsible.
A man with a system.
A man who can close the laptop, turn off the light, settle into the sheets beside a woman he loves, and feel the rare wealth of an unremarkable, ordinary night's sleep.

Dopamine Recalibration — How I Stopped Letting the Feed Think for Me

5:15 AM. Dark bedroom. The phone is warm in my hand, like a loaded gun I'm about to point at my face.

Just ten minutes. A little breathing room before the day breathes down my neck. The lie was so automatic it didn't even register as a lie anymore. It was just Tuesday's first compromise.

Ten minutes became forty. Forty minutes became anxiety about being late. Anxiety became the need to check one more thing to feel better. The loop was so perfect it could've been designed by someone who hates me.

This was Day 1 of what I told myself wasn't a detox or a cleanse or some sanctimonious social media fast. Just a recalibration. A 28-day experiment in not letting the algorithm decide what I think about at 5:15 in the morning.

The Rules (Because I Need Rules)

I deleted nothing. Deletion felt like admitting the apps were stronger than me. Instead, I built a fence:

First, time boundaries: nothing before noon. Nothing after 8 PM. My brain is stupidest at dawn and dusk—why hand it a slot machine during its weakest moments?

Second, service before consumption: Before I could scroll, I had to post something useful to my community. Give before you take. Create before you consume.

Third, ten-minute maximum per session. Not "around ten." Not "ten-ish." Ten. Use a timer like a grown man who knows he can't trust himself.

Fourth, search with intention: Stop letting the feed choose. Ask a specific question. Hunt for specific knowledge. Use the tool instead of letting it use you.

Simple rules. My nervous system had other plans.

The Chemistry Lesson Nobody Asked For

Here's what three years of recovery research taught me: Dopamine isn't the pleasure chemical. It's the "maybe this time" chemical. It doesn't make you happy—it makes you hunt. The scroll isn't satisfying; it's promising that satisfaction is one thumb-flick away.

Every variable reward, every unexpected notification, every perfectly timed controversy—it's all just sophisticated "maybe this time" delivery. Your brain doesn't care that you hate yourself after two hours of scrolling. It only remembers that something might happen if you keep going.

The app makers know this. They have PhDs in this. They turned "maybe this time" into a business model worth billions. And here I was, thinking I could outsmart them with willpower.

Days 1-5: Detox Feels Like Dying

Day 1: Failed before my feet hit the floor. Reached for the phone on autopilot and was doom-scrolling before consciousness fully arrived. Moved the phone to the kitchen that night. You can't fail a test you don't take.

Day 2: Made it to 8:47 AM before the sweats started. Actual sweats. Like my body was withdrawing from a substance. Which, neurologically, it was. Every circuit that expected morning dopamine was filing a complaint. Where's our hit? We had a deal.

Day 3: Posted to my community first, then immediately wanted to check responses. The serve-first rule just moved the addiction five feet to the left. Still progress.

Day 4: Texted a friend: "I'm a 46-year-old man who's sweating because I can't check Instagram." He wrote back: "Same, but TikTok." Shame divided is shame conquered.

Day 5: The physical withdrawal peaked. Felt like mild flu—achy, irritable, exhausted. Googled "social media withdrawal symptoms" on my laptop.

Turns out this is real. Documented. Normal. I wasn't weak. I depended chemically on a notification sound.

Days 6-14: The Flatline

Week 2 was worse than Week 1. The acute withdrawal passed, but what replaced it was worse: nothing. Flat. Gray. Life without the constant micro-hits of novelty felt like eating plain oatmeal forever.

This is when most people quit quitting. When the excitement of the experiment wears off but the benefits haven't shown up yet. When your brain, used to being fed digital cocaine every seven minutes, has to remember how to make its own fun.

Day 8: Realized I hadn't been bored in years. Not truly bored. I'd been filling every micro-moment with stimulation. Waiting in line? Scroll. Commercial break? Scroll. Red light? Scroll. I'd been terrified of empty space.

Day 10: Started to hear my actual thoughts. Turns out, under all that scrolling, I was sad about specific things. Worried about specific problems. The feed hadn't been solving anything—just drowning out the signal.

Day 12: Had a brilliant, stupid idea. Instead of fighting the urge to scroll, I'd honor it—but search for the most boring content possible. Multiplication tables. Phone books from 1987. The history of cement. It made me laugh. It also taught me something: I could use the tool differently. The algorithm wasn't the boss unless I let it be.

Days 15-21: The Turn

Day 15: Woke up differently. Not cured. Not triumphant. Just... clearer. Like someone had cleaned glass I didn't know was dirty. The urge to check was still there, but it had edges now. I could see its shape instead of just being consumed by it.

Started asking a question before each allowed session: "What am I actually looking for?" Connection? Call a friend. Information? Search for it specifically. Entertainment? Watch something actually entertaining, not just addictive. Soothing? The feed is literally the worst possible choice—it agitates, not soothes.

Day 18: Discovered I could be addicted to learning instead of scrolling. I started using my ten-minute windows to research whatever I was curious about. Not random surfing—targeted hunting. The dopamine hit shifted from "something happened" to "I learned something useful."

Day 21: For the first time maybe ever, I used social media and felt better afterward. Posted something helpful. Found specific information I needed. Connected with an old friend. Then, I closed the app at nine minutes and fifty seconds. Not because I had to. Because I was done.

Days 22-28: Integration

The last week wasn't about resistance anymore. It was about design. How do I want to use these tools? What do I want them to do for my life instead of in my life?

Day 24: Started treating the feed like a library instead of a casino. Went in with a question, found answers, took notes, and left. The same mechanism that made me an addict—obsessive focus—could make me a student.

Day 26: Posted something vulnerable about this experiment. The responses were 90% "Thank God someone else is struggling with this too." We're all addicted. We're all ashamed. We're all pretending we're not.

Day 28: Sat down to write what I learned. Ended up outlining this entire book. Not because I conquered social media. Because I learned to dance with it instead of being dragged by it.

What Actually Stuck

The time boundaries stayed. Before noon, my brain isn't ready for the chaos. After 8 PM, it needs to wind down, not up. These aren't restrictions—they're architecture for a life that works.

The serve-first principle became everything. When your first action is giving, the rest of the day reorganizes around contribution instead of consumption. It's not about being noble. It's about reminding yourself that you have something to offer.

The ten-minute cap saved my sanity. Infinite scroll is a river that drowns. Ten minutes is a pond you can wade through.

The intention question—"What am I looking for?"—became muscle memory. It takes three seconds. It changes everything. It's the difference between shopping with a list and wandering the store hungry.

For My Fellow Addicts

If you're reading this while scrolling, I see you. If you've tried to quit seventeen times, I see you. If you feel like a failure because you can't control something designed by teams of neuroscientists to be uncontrollable, I see you.

You're not weak. You're not broken. You're just fighting a battle with the wrong weapons. Willpower versus algorithm is like bringing a knife to a drone strike.

Build fences. Use timers. Tell someone. Expect withdrawal. Expect the flatline. Expect Day 15 to feel different. Expect to fail and count that as data, not defeat.

Most importantly, you don't have to quit. You have to restructure. The goal isn't to become someone who doesn't use social media. The goal is to become someone who uses it instead of being used by it.

The Ten-Minute Truth

This experiment didn't make me pure. It made me honest. I'm still an addict. I just chose a better addiction. Instead of being addicted to the scroll, I'm addicted to the constraint. Instead of chasing "maybe this time," I'm chasing "what can I learn in ten minutes?"

The feed will never love you back. It will never have enough. It will never tell you to stop. That's your job. That's the work. That's the practice.

Start tomorrow. Set a timer. Ten minutes. Ask what you're looking for. Close the app when the timer goes off, even if—especially if—you want just one more scroll.

The algorithm doesn't have to change. You do.

One ten-minute window at a time.

Snow Wars: When You Know You're Home

The storm arrived like a prank from a kinder universe—eight inches overnight in a Tennessee town that usually gets dust, not drifts. The cul-de-sac went quiet and bright, the kind of quiet you hear only when the world is padded and forgiven. It should've just been a snow day. It turned out to be a mirror.

Inside, the house held all the old seams. Newlyweds in our fifties learning each other's rhythms. Three strong-willed girls with histories and opinions that could power a small nation. Kelly—calm, precise, kind—finding her footing in a home where sarcasm is a second language and snacks are a currency. Jenna straddling two worlds, half-packed for a future that makes your throat tight. Livvie navigating middle school like an ambassador to a warring country. Emmy, the former "woman of the house," handing over invisible keys she'd held since it was just the two of us, wondering who she was without the clipboard.

There was a time a day like this would've been an excuse. I know the timestamp of my old life by the smell. Gas station coffee and air freshener at 2:12 a.m. The tight chest and busy jaw. From seventeen to twenty, I chased the comet—cocaine turning nights into thin, bright wire. You don't forget that speed, or how it rents your soul by the hour. I kicked it, and the hunger shape-shifted. Paper magazines hidden under mattresses. Then the internet arrived and the hiding got easier, the shame more efficient. Years of that—until 2020, when I finally took my hands off the toxic steering wheel and said it out loud.

The hunger didn't disappear; it negotiated. It found new alleyways. The phone made a perfect pharmacy. Infinite novelty, dopamine drips, nostalgia in high definition. I learned to dock it in the hallway like a dangerous pet. Five seconds. Close the tab. Put it away. Breathe. Call a man who knows my voice when it's lying.

I could tell you now that I was beyond all that when the snow came. That would be a prettier story. The truth is, the house was warm and the kitchen light was soft, and the phone buzzed with a message that tugged an old thread. Not a person—just an algorithm serving me memory. I felt the tiny tilt—the one I know too well. The one that used to pull whole nights into a drain. Five seconds, I told myself. Dock. Walk away. I did.

When I stepped outside, Kevin was already alive—coal eyes, carrot nose, my *Washington Commanders* beanie smirking at me from a head that didn't earn it. The dogs were wild, the air medicinal, the girls loading snow like they meant it. Kelly stood in the center of the yard with the look she gets when her childhood finds her again—head back, eyes bright, hair stuck to her cheeks. She saw me and grinned with the kind of mischief that feels like an invitation and a dare.

It started with false confidence: Kelly and me versus all three girls. Original team versus the natives. We lobbed soft arcs, pretending we cared about strategy while we scoped each other's throws. Then Kelly betrayed me with the casual cruelty of switching allegiances mid-throw— "Girls versus guys!" she shrieked, nailing me with a perfect shot to the shoulder before running to join my daughters. Four on one. The math was clear. I was doomed.

I ran and dodged and realized I'm not nearly as fast as the man I used to be. And I was glad. The old speed took; this slowness gives. There's a holiness in getting pelted by your own children. Every thump was a sacrament. Every squeal of "Get him!" baptized a corner of the house we'd been circling carefully for months.

We forgot everything for an hour. The black hole of college applications. The text that didn't come from a maybe-friend. The tight-lipped way we sometimes avoid the topic that sits in the middle of the table and eats our patience. We forgot who belonged to whom first. We forgot to be careful.

Snow has a way of making you honest. It sticks where it lands. You can see the path you took. You can see where you fell. Face-down in a drift, my mitten raised in theatrical surrender, I thought about another kind of white—powder measured on a key, lines on a bathroom counter in a house I try not to drive by. I thought about God as a patient father, and about how many times I chose relief that charged interest. I thought about 2020, the year I asked my secrets to go live somewhere else.

We piled into the car the way families do when they've done something elemental. Wet denim, steamed-up windows, the smell of wool and dog. Jenna's makeup did that mascara river thing and she didn't care. Livvie's hair went punk-rock icicle. Emmy, suddenly without a role to supervise, hooked her elbow through Kelly's like she'd always known where to put it. Kelly's hat sacrificed to Kevin, snow melting down her neck; she let it run.

We dripped our way into the mall like a poorly planned performance art piece. Sensible people stared. We ate greasy food and told war stories. "Did you see Dad's face when we all hit him at once?" "I thought his eyebrows were going to fly off." I laughed because they were right. I laughed because I had eyebrows to lose. There was a time I would have been too hungover or too far gone or too busy doomscrolling to be a target.

Here's the thing: I haven't become a different species. I'm the same man with reordered loves. I still like intensity; I just pick better altars. I'm addicted on purpose now—to early lights-out, to training sessions that make my hands shake clean, to the cold shock that reminds me I have a body I don't have to punish to feel. I'm addicted to service—Thursday half-hours with divorced dads who text from outside bars at 11:07 PM and need a sentence that gets them home. I'm addicted to the click of the phone docking at 9:45, to the way gratitude can turn down the volume on scarcity in two minutes flat. These are obsessions I chose because my life asked for guardrails and I got tired of pretending I could fly.

Old me would've taken that snow day as a margin to drift—sneak something, scroll something, stir up a little chaos to feel alive. The old me loved beginnings and eruptions, hated maintenance. Old me mistook intensity for intimacy and attention for love. Old me would have been the funniest guy in the room and the loneliest at the end of the night. Old me would have stayed on the porch checking a thread that promised a hit of the past while the present flung joy at my empty chair.

New me is boring in the best way. He docks the phone and steps into the yard. He lets four girls obliterate him with frozen joy because he understands something he didn't before: presence is a pleasure that doesn't invoice you later. He chooses slow on purpose. He builds routines that survive grumpy moods and thin sleep. He says, "I'm defensive; give me ten," and means it. He apologizes while the tea is still warm. He's more impressed by a Tuesday night at home than a Saturday on a stage.

If you're reading this and feeling the tug of your own old neighborhood—whatever its drug of choice—hear me: you don't have to become someone else to come home. You have to aim for what you already are. The part of you that loves the rush can love the run, the ice bath, the deep work block, the daring conversation. The part of you that loved the secret can learn to love the text you send that says, "Wobbling. Docked. Safe." The part of you that kept a stash can keep a Rolodex—therapists, sponsors, friends who answer on the second ring.

On the way back from lunch, the sun did that thing winter suns do—low and gold, striking the snow at an angle that makes your house look like it was painted by someone with a crush on you. We turned into our street and the girls started arguing about who had the best throwing arm. I thought, without effort, this is mine. Not in the way that clutches, in the way that finally exhales. The house didn't look different. The driveway was still a mess. Kevin still wore my Commanders beanie like he paid for season tickets. But everything felt rearranged inside me. The craving for elsewhere went quiet.

Home, I've learned, isn't where your packages get delivered. It's where your addictions lose their alibi. It's where you stop performing for the people who know your worst stories and start living in front of them anyway. It's where you get your face rearranged by snowballs thrown by girls who trust you enough to aim for your head. It's where you raise a mitten, surrender dramatically, and let yourself be loved.

I used to need five seconds to ruin a night. Now I use five seconds to choose one. That's not heroism; that's plumbing. That's putting the valves in the right place so the pressure moves water to the rooms that need it. If I have a secret weapon, it's that I stopped arguing with gravity and started building rails. I didn't become less of a man. I became a man who can stand still while joy finds him.

We watched a movie that night and made it twenty minutes. We slept in a heap of blankets and damp socks and a dog. Somewhere around midnight, I woke to the soft chorus of a house breathing. I reached for my phone. Habit. Hunger. Five seconds. I smiled in the dark at my own hand, empty. The hallway dock glowed like a small lighthouse. I rolled toward Kelly and put my face in her hair, which smelled like clean wool and melting ice. I thought of seventeen-year-old me, bright and brittle, so sure that more was the only way through. I wanted to tell him about this moment, about the ridiculous hat on a snowman, about the girls who don't share blood but share laughter, about the way surrender sometimes feels like victory.

When you know you're home, the wars don't end. You just pick better ones. Not the kind you fight alone in bathrooms and browsers. The kind you fight in yards with people who will drive you to the mall soaking wet and roast you in the food court with love. You lose this kind on purpose because losing earns an invitation. The kind that ends with everyone asleep mid-plot, a pile of humans and dogs, the heat kicking on, the storm spent, the house making those old wood sounds that say, Stay.

Here's to the snow wars. To the men who used to run hot and far and now sit down in their own living rooms. To the old me who taught the new me what not to worship. To the obsessions I retired and the ones I keep on purpose. To five seconds that changed everything, again and again, until it sticks.

If you're still out there circling, come in. Dock the phone. Step into the yard. Let yourself get hit.

You'll know you're home when you stop keeping score and start keeping company. When the snow melts and the beanie slides down Kevin's face and the driveway turns back to ordinary, you'll still have it—the sound of your family choosing you back. That sound will carry you through the next storm, and the next. It already is.

The architecture in this book isn't magic. It's scaffolding for a single truth: You can redirect any hunger toward something that feeds instead of devours. Every system, every protocol, every framework—they're all just different ways of saying the same thing: Point your obsession at something worth being obsessed with. Your intensity isn't the problem. Where you aim it is everything.

Tomorrow morning, you'll wake up with the same brain that got you into trouble. Good. That's the same brain that can lock onto morning light, cold water, hard work, true words, and the sound of someone you love laughing at your terrible jokes. The part of you that could chase a high for seventeen hours straight? That's the part that can protect a deep work block like your life depends on it. Because it does.

The math remains simple: Every addiction is a love story pointed in the wrong direction. Turn it around. Point it home.

Start with five seconds. Just five. The space between impulse and action. Between the itch and the scratch. Between who you were and who you're becoming. In those five seconds, everything changes. Not because you become someone new, but because you remember who you've always been underneath the hunger.

You're not broken. You're just aiming wrong.

Aim better.

Start now.

You don't have to do this work alone.

If reading this book stirred something — clarity, discomfort, curiosity, or a desire for support — scan the QR code below to explore additional resources, live integration experiences, and the **BetterIn3.com** **community**.

These spaces exist to help you stay with the work over time, in a way that feels grounded, honest, and sustainable.

No pressure.
Just support, if and when it's useful.

About the Author

Thomas Goddard is an award-winning actor, designer, author, story coach, and recovering addict whose life's work is shaped by the same transformation he now teaches. At 17, Thomas fell into a cocaine addiction, a battle that would shadow decades of his life and ultimately lead him to the healing, clarity, and purpose he carries today. Now 53—and feeling younger, stronger, and more alive than ever—Thomas has dedicated himself to helping others break free from the loops that keep them stuck, exhausted, and disconnected from the life they deserve.

After navigating two divorces, the challenges of single fatherhood, and the journey of raising two daughters in separate homes, Thomas learned what it means to show up without perfection—just honesty, presence, and grit. Those experiences, combined with his evolution into a father of five in a beautifully blended family with his wife Kelly and her daughters Jenna, Linda, and Laura, form the heart of his work. His stories come from lived experience: heartbreak, recovery, rebuilding, and the relentless commitment to love better.

Thomas is the founder of **BetterIn3.com**, where he works with neurodivergent adults—especially those who have spent years masking, over-functioning, and burning out while trying to meet impossible expectations. His signature *ReliableMomentum^{TM}* system helps clients create clarity, confidence, and calm even on the days they're running at 20%. His approach is built on compassion, science, lived neurodivergent experience, and a fundamental belief that every person deserves a life that *fits* them, not a life they have to contort themselves to fit into.

As an author, Thomas writes from the trenches with a blend of humor, humility, and raw truth. His book **Five Seconds That Changed Everything: A Secret Weapon Every Dad Needs in His Arsenal** is a collection of short stories from his two failed marriages, his years as a single dad to Emmy and Livvie, the mistakes he made, the lessons he learned, and the five-second mindset shifts that helped him become a present and resilient father. It also chronicles the unexpected joy of finding his partner, lover, and now-wife Kelly, even in the middle of chasing his entrepreneurial dreams.

His upcoming book, **The Conformity Loop** (scheduled for spring, 2026), explores the spectrum between authenticity and assimilation, and how masking and "fitting in" can silently erode identity, energy, and joy. It is the second book in his *Behavior Loop* series, following the deeply personal and widely resonant **Addiction Loop**, which unpacks how addictive patterns form, hide, and heal in the lives of everyday people.

When he's not writing, coaching, or building systems that make life easier for neurodivergent professionals, Thomas collaborates with creatives in Chattanooga, Tennessee, helping people share their stories to build connection, belonging, and community across dividing lines.

Through every project, role, and chapter of his life, Thomas remains committed to one guiding principle:

Success isn't about perfection—it's about presence, courage, and finding new ways to love this life a little better every day.

Endnotes and References

Prologue

- Concept: Addiction as predictable neuro-learning loops; dopamine as incentive salience (wanting vs liking).
- Source: Berridge & Robinson (1998; 2008); Koob & Volkow (2016).
- Endnote: "On dopamine as incentive salience and the 'wanting vs liking' distinction, see Berridge & Robinson (1998; 2008). For addiction neurocircuitry, see Koob & Volkow (2016)."
- Refs: as listed.

Chapter 1 — The Universal Addict

- Concept: Habit loop structure (cue → craving → ritual → reward → learning).
- Source: Duhigg (2012) popularized loop framing; Wood & Rünger (2016) for habit science.
- Endnote: "For the habit loop framing, see Duhigg (2012); for contemporary habit research, see Wood & Rünger (2016)."
- Concept: Prediction engine/anticipatory dopamine spikes.
- Source: Schultz (1997); Wise (2004).
- Endnote: "On prediction error and anticipatory dopamine activity, see Schultz (1997); Wise (2004)."

Chapter 2 — The Brain and Body on Addiction

- Concept: Wanting vs liking, tolerance/sensitization, novelty effects.
- Source: Robinson & Berridge (2003); Robinson & Berridge (2008).
- Endnote: "On wanting vs liking and incentive sensitization, see Robinson & Berridge (2003; 2008)."
- Concept: State/context-dependent triggers.

- Source: Tulving & Thomson (1973).
- Endnote: "On encoding specificity and state/context-dependent recall, see Tulving & Thomson (1973)."
- Concept: Morning/mid-morning executive function vs late-night vulnerability; sleep/blue light.
- Source: Czeisler (2013); AASM guidance.
- Endnote: "On circadian rhythms, sleep, and light exposure, see Czeisler (2013); AASM guidance."

Chapter 3 — Short-Form and the State-Change Escape Hatch

- Concept: Variable rewards, infinite scroll, autoplay, design patterns that extend sessions.
- Source: Eyal (2014) on triggers/action/variable reward; Alter (2017) on persuasive tech; Harris/Center for Humane Technology.
- Endnote: "On variable rewards and persuasive tech design, see Eyal (2014); Alter (2017); Center for Humane Technology."
- Concept: Attention fragmentation; task switching.
- Source: Gazzaley & Rosen (2016); Mark (2023).
- Endnote: "On attention fragmentation and task switching in digital environments, see Gazzaley & Rosen (2016); Mark (2023)."

Sidebar: Dopamine Recalibration

- Concept: Withdrawal-like symptoms with social media reduction; mood "flatline," novelty/anticipation.
- Source: Lembke (2021) for clinical framing; Montag & Pontes (2018) for problematic use associations.
- Endnote: "For clinical perspectives on dopamine balance and withdrawal-like phenomena with behavioral addictions, see Lembke (2021); see also Montag & Pontes (2018)."

Chapter 4 — Tired Scrolling

- Concept: Triadic model (impulsive, reflective, interoceptive) and phone presence's effect on conversation quality.
- Sources: Turel & Bechara (2016); Przybylski & Weinstein (2013); Wilmer et al. (2017).
- Endnote: "On problematic internet/smartphone use and cognition/relationships, see Turel & Bechara (2016); Przybylski & Weinstein (2013); Wilmer et al. (2017)."

Chapter 5 — Congruence vs Compulsion

- Concept: Meaning/purpose as navigational aid.
- Source: Frankl (1959).
- Endnote: "On purpose as a buffer against despair and compulsion, see Frankl (1959)."

Chapter 6 — Counterfeit Connection

- Concept: Betrayal trauma; safety before closeness; repair and boundaries.
- Sources: Freyd (1996); Gottman & Gottman (2015); Johnson (2019).
- Endnote: "On betrayal trauma and relational repair processes, see Freyd (1996); Gottman & Gottman (2015); Johnson (2019)."

Chapter 7 — Invisible Recovery

- Concept: "Tell it first, don't fix it first"; stages of change; motivational interviewing stance.
- Sources: Prochaska & DiClemente (1983); Miller & Rollnick (2012); Steffens & Means (partners' trauma) or Carnes (sexual compulsivity).
- Endnote: "For stages of change and the MI stance (collaboration, evocation, autonomy), see Prochaska & DiClemente (1983); Miller & Rollnick (2012). For partners' trauma, see Steffens & Means (2015)."

Chapter 8 — Work, Willpower, and the Myth of Control

- Concept: Environment > willpower; deep work blocks; effort valuation.
- Sources: Newport (2016); Westbrook & Braver (2015); Mark (2023).
- Endnote: "On designing for deep work and the neuroeconomics of cognitive effort, see Newport (2016); Westbrook & Braver (2015)."

Chapter 9 — Fatherhood, Divorce, and Distance

- Concept: Child outcomes under shared custody and father involvement.
- Sources: Nielsen (2014); Lamb (2012); Amato (2010).
- Endnote: "On shared custody and the importance of father involvement, see Nielsen (2014); Lamb (2012); Amato (2010)."

Chapter 10 — Early Recovery: Surfing Urges

- Concept: Urge surfing; brief breathing protocols; witness-first.
- Sources: Marlatt & Gordon (1985); Bowen et al. (2010); Kabat-Zinn (1990).
- Endnote: "On urge surfing and mindfulness-based relapse prevention, see Marlatt & Gordon (1985); Bowen et al. (2010)."

Chapter 11 — Alone Together

- Concept: Energy as precondition; mind-wandering unhappy; ego depletion debate.
- Sources: Killingsworth & Gilbert (2010); Inzlicht & Schmeichel (2012).
- Endnote: "On mind-wandering/affect, see Killingsworth & Gilbert (2010); on self-control/'ego depletion' debates, see Inzlicht & Schmeichel (2012)."

Chapter 12 — Addicted to the Right Things

- Concept: Re-aiming the reward system; environmental design for eating.
- Sources: Gardner (2011); Wansink (2014, with replication caveats).
- Endnote: "On reward/anti-reward systems and re-aiming reinforcement, see Gardner (2011). On kitchen environment design, see Wansink (2014), noting replication concerns."

Chapter 13 — Truth Culture at Home

- Concept: Repair scripts; "try again"; Sunday summit.
- Sources: Gottman & Silver (1999); Lerner (2017); Siegel & Bryson (2011).
- Endnote: "On repair, soft-startups, and family emotional regulation, see Gottman & Silver (1999); Lerner (2017); Siegel & Bryson (2011)."

Chapter 14 — Think Clean to Live Clean

- Concept: 7 Elements and 8 Standards of Critical Thinking.
- Source: Paul & Elder (2006).
- Suggested handling: If you want to use their phrasing verbatim, add quotation marks around the list and cite. Otherwise, keep paraphrased and attribute. Example endnote: "Framework adapted from Paul & Elder (2006)."
- Concept: System 1/System 2.
- Source: Kahneman (2011).
- Endnote: "On fast/slow thinking modes, see Kahneman (2011)."

Chapter 15 — High Performance Habits for Recovery

- Concept: High Performance Habits (Clarity, Energy, Courage, Productivity, Influence); PQO.
- Source: Burchard (2017).
- Endnote: "Adapted from Burchard's High Performance Habits (2017), esp. PQO and weekly review structures."

Chapter 16 — From Recovery to Purpose

- Concept: Service as a recovery lever predicting outcomes.
- Source: Pagano et al. (2009); AA service tradition.
- Endnote: "On helping others and long-term sobriety outcomes, see Pagano et al. (2009)."

Chapter 17 — Heretic's Playbook + 30-Day Plan

- Concept: 5-second initiation; tiny steps; behavior = motivation × ability × prompt.
- Sources: Robbins (2017) for countdown; Fogg (2009; 2019) for tiny behaviors and B=MAP.
- Endnote: "On 5-second initiation, see Robbins (2017). On tiny behaviors and triggers (B=MAP), see Fogg (2009; 2019)."

Chapter 18 / Epilogue — Ordinary Joy

- Concept: Broaden-and-build; flourishing.
- Sources: Fredrickson (2001); Seligman (2011).
- Endnote: "On positive emotions broadening attention and building resources, see Fredrickson (2001); on well-being and practices that sustain it, see Seligman (2011)."